PEW RIGHTS

PEW RIGHTS

For People Who Listen to Sermons

Roger E. Van Harn

WILLIAM B. EERDMANS PUBLISHING COMPANY
GRAND RAPIDS, MICHIGAN

Library of Congress Cataloging-in-Publication Data

Van Harn, Roger, 1932-
Pew rights : for people who listen to sermons /
by Roger E. Van Harn.
p.   cm.
Includes bibliographical references.
ISBN 0-8028-3704-2
1. Preaching.   I. Title.
BV4211.2.V34   1992
251 — dc20   92-6286
                                        CIP

The Scripture quotations in this publication are taken from the Revised Standard Version of the Bible, copyrighted 1946, 1952 © 1971, 1973 by the Division of Christian Education of the National Council of Churches of Christ in the U.S.A., and used by permission.

Parts of Chapter 3 appeared in a different form in "Covenantalize the World; Evangelize the Church," an article that appeared serially in *Calvinist Contact* in 1985, in the June 14 and 21 and July 5 issues. The author and publisher gratefully acknowledge permission for the use of this material.

We also wish to thank Augsburg-Fortress Publications for permission to reprint Herbert F. Brokering's poem "Sermon," from *Uncovered Feelings* (Philadelphia: Fortress Press, 1966), pp. 24-25.

Contents

PART IV: . . . TO HEAR THE WORD OF GOD

*This book is for Grace Church,
where a gathering of people
that resembles the kingdom of God
has listened with me
for fifteen years.*

Foreword

ROGER E. VAN HARN is a gifted preacher and pastor
who has written and preached many sermons in his years
of ministry. In this book, however, he has chosen not to
stand in his customary place in the pulpit but to sit in the
pew. He is well acquainted with what it means for a
preacher to be commissioned to preach. Now he turns his
attention to what it means for the congregation to be
commissioned to hear. Only when preachers know what
the church has the right to hear, he maintains, can they
truly know what they are called to proclaim.

It is both strange and unfortunate that books on
preaching can often be eloquent about the tasks of the
preacher but largely silent about the role of the congregation. Perhaps this is due simply to the toxic smog of cler-
icalism. Perhaps it is the lingering effect of Protestant
Word-of-God theologies grown old, taken out of the communities and crises that gave them life and placed in the
nursing homes of seminary textbooks, their categories now
abstract and hardened. Or maybe it is simply a product of
the illusion that, since preaching ministers do all the talk-

ing, they do all the real work. For whatever reasons, it is only in the last few years that homileticians have begun to recover what the New Testament writers knew quite well: the lively and interactive role of hearing in the preaching event. Only lately have we witnessed a restoration of the awareness that the hearing of a sermon requires as much energy, imagination, and faithful responsibility as the preaching of one. This book is a sign of that recovery.

In one sense Van Harn begins not with preaching but with baptism. He starts not with the sermon but by considering the community in which such extraordinary speech occurs, the people of God set apart in baptism — in essence, ordained — to a new identity and a particular mission in the world. If this congregational identity and mission are to be nourished and strengthened in and through preaching, then the preacher must be aware of their needs, or, as Van Harn phrases it, their "rights."

As he develops an inventory of the rights of sermon listeners and their accompanying responsibilities, Van Harn builds a strong and many-layered doctrine of the church. He urges the church to refresh its memory of God's ongoing story, to live out its role in that story, and, thus, to live as a challenge to and a comfort for the world.

If this book has a single goal, it is to encourage preachers to listen to the hearers, to listen to the hearers as *church*. When preachers listen to the church, they are reminded that the church has heard the gospel before and been shaped by it. The church has a kerygmatic memory, sometimes faulty and always in need of refreshment, but a gospel-shaped memory nonetheless. If preachers listen *before* they preach, they will know where that memory is strong and where it is weak, and they will create sermons more effectively tailored to build up the Body of Christ. If they listen *as* they preach, they will be more faithful to the dialogical character of the gospel itself. If they also listen *after* they preach, they will be humbled by the frailty of their sermonic words while, at the same time, awed by the ways in which the Word takes root and grows in the lives of faithful people.

Princeton Theological Seminary   THOMAS G. LONG

Preface

"PEW RIGHTS? How do you spell it?"

"Just like it sounds: Pew rights."

"Do you mean 'Rites?' R-i-t-e-s?"

"No, I'm thinking about pew rights, as in civil rights."

"Never heard of them. Are you sure there are any?"

That conversation is typical of many that I have had in the past eight years while I have been studying and reflecting on the subject. Such talks commonly result in two questions: Are there pew rights? and Would a person who spends more time in the pulpit than in the pew know anything about them?

The answer to both questions is yes. There are pew rights, and a person who preaches sermons should know something about them.

Rights, after all, are rooted in responsibilities. Civil rights are rooted in social responsibilities. Children's rights are rooted in parental responsibilities. Patient rights are rooted in medical responsibilities. And pew rights are rooted in pulpit responsibilities.

Much attention has been paid to pulpit responsibility

in the past twenty years. Good books have tumbled from the press signaling a renewed interest in preaching in almost every Christian tradition. Nearly every book on preaching gives significant attention to the pulpit-pew relationship. Such titles as John R. W. Stott's *Between Two Worlds* and F. Dean Lueking's *Preaching: The Art of Connecting God and People* indicate the concern contained in nearly every book on preaching. Some of the books have gone farther and paid attention to the pulpit-pew partnership — Reuel Howe's *Partners in Preaching*, for instance, and Martin E. Marty's *The Word: People Participating in Preaching*. Not many have focused on listening to sermons from the pew. William D. Thompson's *Listener's Guide to Preaching* was an early exception, and J. Randall Nichols concluded his book *Building the Word* with a chapter entitled "A Bill of Rights for Congregations."

Insofar as the pew rights identified in this book are rooted in pulpit responsibilities, it contains nothing that cannot be found in one form or another in the many good books on that subject that have appeared in the last twenty years. However, because this book casts pulpit responsibilities into the form of pew rights — which they indeed are — it offers the people who listen to sermons some guidance about what they have a right to expect.

My impression across the years is that many people who listen to sermons have vague impressions about what they should be hearing, but they lack clarity and confidence in speaking about it. I hope this book serves to put some of those intuitions into words and to hone their expectations in faithful ways.

The reader should be aware, however, that rights that are rooted in the responsibilities of others will entail responsibilities when they are claimed. There will be times in reading some of these chapters that "pew rights" will sound very much like "pew responsibilities." I am not sorry about that. In ways we do not yet fully understand, rights and responsibilites both belong to the dignity God intends for us. Pew rights are rooted in pulpit responsibilities, and when we claim those rights, we will find pew responsibilities coming with them.

I am deeply indebted to Grace Christian Reformed Church of Grand Rapids, Michigan, for granting me study leaves periodically from 1983 to 1991. I began my specialized studies in homiletics at Trinity Lutheran Seminary, Columbus, Ohio, in the early to mid-1970s. In 1983 a six-month study leave allowed me to spend the fall quarter at Princeton Theological Seminary as a visiting fellow — thanks to the grace of President Thomas Gillespie. While there, Professor Thomas G. Long challenged, tested, and encouraged me until I developed a valid focus. And Professor Cullen Story interrupted himself almost daily to offer questions, suggestions, and help.

Members of Grace Church, fellow listeners with me, have made this work possible not only by granting me study leaves but also through their steady encouragement. Edward Ericson, Jr., and Gordon Van Harn, both of Calvin College and Grace Church, read my earliest attempts to identify pew rights and urged me to proceed. William B. Eerdmans, Jr., and Sam Eerdmans, both of the William B. Eerdmans Publishing Company and Grace Church, were patient with my delays and undaunted by my difficulties. Ray and Lillian Grissen were generous in providing their cottage overlooking Upper Silver Lake in northern Michigan, where I retreated to read, reflect, and write. With and behind these people is the wonderfully diverse and often unpredictable family of God that is Grace Church. For fifteen years we have listened together as though our life depended on it — as indeed it does.

I am also grateful to my family and my children's families for participating in the life of Grace Church and for supporting my work. From earliest days in the ministry, I trained my wife, Ellie, and children, Karen, Karl, Paul, Roger, Philip, and Thomas, to say "great sermon" whenever I needed it. And it always helped, even if it was more an expression of love than truth.

This book is written for people who listen to sermons and also read books. However, should this book fall into the hands of someone who preaches sermons, or if the reader knows a preacher who could use some advice, here is a long-neglected gem from Martin Luther's *Table Talk:*

> Conrad Cordatus said to Dr. Martin Luther, "Reverend Father, teach me in a brief way how to preach."
>
> Luther responded briefly, "First, you must learn to go up to the pulpit. Second, you must know that you should stay there for a time. Third, you must learn to get down again."
>
> He added nothing in addition to these words, and as a result Cordatus was quite angry. Yet at length it occurred to him that the doctor had hit the mark very well. Anybody who keeps this order will be a good preacher.[1]

Blessed are the sermon listeners who pass this counsel to their preacher, and blessed are the preachers who follow it.

---

1. Luther, *Table Talk,* vol. 54 of *Luther's Works,* ed. and trans. Theodore G. Tappert (Philadelphia: Fortress Press, 1967), no. 5171b.

— PART I —

We Listen to Sermons . . .

— 1 —

Where Would You Like to Sit?

"GOOD MORNING! Welcome to our church. It looks like there are five of you. Is there a place where you prefer to sit?"

"Is there a place toward the back on that side?"

"I think so. Right this way, please."

People do develop preferences for where they sit when they go to worship. In some churches — especially Protestant churches — regular worshipers often establish "squatters rights" to a certain pew. Gone are the days when members bought their right to a pew with money, but in many churches today, long and faithful use of the same pew earns the right to use it by unspoken agreement.

Choices about where to sit when we worship are probably shaped by many factors. Familiarity or unfamiliarity with the place, the size of the group or family we are with, personal needs or temperament, and perhaps even what we believe about what happens in worship can influence our preferences. James Dittes found meaning and significance in how people traditionally behave when they enter the church. In some churches persons begin worship by crossing themselves, kneeling, or praying immediately

3

upon entering. In other churches, however, worshipers head immediately for the vacant pew nearest the rear and chat sociably with their neighbors.[1] Regardless of how and why our preferences get shaped, greeters and ushers usually try to respect them.

Though it may be personally important to us where we like to sit or stand when we worship, on a deeper level we know that it does not matter. Wherever we sit in the church building and listen to a sermon in worship, we are sitting in a special place. Rightly understood, when we listen to a sermon *we have the right to sit at the center of the church's mission.*

This pew right is based on St. Paul's mission order for the church recorded in Romans 10:13-17:

> "Every one who calls upon the name of the Lord will be saved." But how are men to call upon him in whom they have not believed? And how are they to believe in him of whom they have never heard? And how are they to hear without a preacher? And how can men preach unless they are sent? . . . So faith comes from what is heard, and what is heard comes by the preaching of Christ.

These words are often read at a service of ordination in which the church commissions a person to preach the gospel of Christ. Appropriate as that is, if we use these words to direct our attention to the pulpit where the preaching happens, we miss the central message of St. Paul's mission order. He draws our attention to the purpose of preaching — namely, the *hearing* of Christ. Because faith

---

1. See Dittes, *Church in the Way* (New York: Scribner, 1967), p. 332.

comes by hearing, he gives hearing the central place in the church's mission order:

Sending — Preaching — *Hearing* — Believing — Calling

The whole mission order includes a church order and a salvation order. The church order is composed of sending, preaching, and hearing. The salvation order is composed of hearing, believing, and calling on the name of the Lord. The mission order joins the church order and the salvation order in the event of *hearing*. Hearing stands at the center between preaching and believing. It fulfills the purpose of the sending and makes possible our calling on the name of the Lord.

Because hearing is the event that stands between the purpose of the church and the experience of salvation, between preaching and believing, it is easily overlooked. But because it is central in St. Paul's mission order, we may say that when we listen to a sermon, *we have the right to sit at the center of the church's mission.*

To say that hearing is central in the church's mission is not to say that it is the *whole* mission, however. The sending, preaching, believing, and calling on the name of the Lord are essential. Nor is it to say that hearing is superior to the other elements. But hearing "the word of faith" (Rom. 10:8) or "the preaching of Christ" (Rom. 10:17) stands at the center of the mission between speaking (preaching) and believing.

In a Protestant church I know of, the congregation was deeply invested financially and emotionally in building a new house of worship. One of the points that was debated involved the location of the chancel furnishings. Should there be a central pulpit? Should there be a chancel

divided between lectern and pulpit with the table centered?
And what should be done with the baptismal font? Argu-
ments from the faith and history of the church were intense.
The debate resulted in a standoff that was settled by a close
vote.

With all due respect for that debate, I am asking a
different question in this book: What belongs in the center
of the church's mission — the pulpit or the pew? According
to St. Paul's mission order, the pulpit was made for the
pew, not the pew for the pulpit.

Paul's mission order makes explicit what was present
from the beginning: hearing stands between God's speaking
and his people's trusting. Adam and Eve hid among the
trees because they heard the Lord God walking in the
garden in the cool of the day (Gen. 3:8). But when God
asked the searching question "Where are you?" a new kind
of hearing happened. Hearing the question brought them
out of hiding into the beginning of trust.

Hearing God's saving message has a history among
God's people. When Moses returned to Egypt after being
banished to Midian for killing an Egyptian, he and Aaron met
with the elders of Israel. They told the elders that God knew
what was happening and would deliver them from Pharaoh.
What happened? "The people believed; and when they heard
that the LORD had visited the people of Israel and that he had
seen their affliction, they bowed their heads and worshiped"
(Exod. 4:31). And when the prophet spoke to the beleaguered
people of Israel who were still staggering from the effects of
the exile in Babylon, what did he say? "Have you not known?
Have you not heard? The LORD is the everlasting God, the
Creator of the ends of the earth. He does not faint or grow
weary, his understanding is unsearchable. . . . Listen to me in
silence . . ." (Isa. 40:28, 41:1).

St. Paul himself had heard a voice on the road to Damascus that changed him from a persecutor of the church to an apostle. He knew that because of the death and resurrection of Jesus and the coming of the Holy Spirit, the history of hearing God's message had entered a new day. It was now the age of the gospel for all the nations: "For there is no distinction between Jew and Greek; the same Lord is Lord of all and bestows his riches upon all who call upon him" (Rom. 10:12). Faith had always come from what was heard, but a new age for hearing had arrived in Christ. Now "what is heard comes by the preaching of Christ" for all the nations (Rom. 10:17).

But hearing the preaching of Christ does not always bring about believing immediately, fully, or permanently. When the message of God is heard, it may collide with cherished beliefs and trigger resistance or rejection. An important moment in the history of hearing the preaching of Christ came when Christ preached in his own hometown of Nazareth. Luke reports what Jesus said and did, describes the reaction of the people, and more than suggests that in Jesus Christ the hearing of God's message had entered a new age:

> And he came to Nazareth, where he had been brought up; and he went to the synagogue, as his custom was, on the sabbath day. And he stood up to read; and there was given to him the book of the prophet Isaiah. He opened the book and found the place where it was written,
>
> > "The Spirit of the Lord is upon me,
> > because he has anointed me to preach good news
> >   to the poor.
> > He has sent me to proclaim release to the captives
> > and recovering of sight to the blind,

to set at liberty those who are oppressed,
to proclaim the acceptable year of the Lord. "

And he closed the book, and gave it back to the
attendant, and sat down; and the eyes of all in the synagogue were fixed on him. And he began to say to them,
"Today this scripture has been fulfilled in your hearing."
(Luke 4:16-21)

Before Jesus began to preach, those who attended the
synagogue regularly had some pretty strong ideas about
what they were likely to hear. They were familiar with the
way "sermons" went in the synagogue. Jesus would speak
from this passage about how the exile of Israel in Babylon
came to an end because God once again delivered them.
As it was in the deliverance from Egypt, so it was again in
the rescue from exile, and so it would be again some day.
God had remembered his promise, loosed their bonds, and
restored their fortunes. In the strength of telling the story,
Jesus would brighten the hope for a new deliverance from
Rome. Jesus would calm the restless, instruct the faithful,
and inspire the downhearted.

But Jesus shocked them. His sermon was different:
"Today this scripture has been fulfilled in your hearing."
No one could have expected it. Saying that a scripture had
been fulfilled that very day because they heard *him* read it
was like saying that the Messiah had come to them that
day in the synagogue. But Jesus was just a hometown boy.
They spoke well of him only until it dawned on them what
he had done when he preached his nine-word sermon about
a scripture being fulfilled the moment they heard him read
it. Jesus had brought about a crisis of faith for them.

Their wondering turned to questioning and then to
outrage. When Jesus added a postscript to the sermon

about how God showed great mercy to two "outsiders," a widow of Sidon and a leper of Syria, the jury brought in the verdict: Jesus would have to be silenced to preserve the scriptures and protect the faith.

When Jesus preached his sermon in the synagogue, the hearing of God's Word entered a new age. No longer would Israel's hope of salvation be sustained only by memories kept alive by the scriptures in the synagogue. Their hopes could rest in the person of this Jesus of Nazareth, who fulfilled the scriptures in their hearing and ushered them into a new age. Never had Isaiah the prophet been interpreted like this. And as if to add insult to injury, Jesus omitted the next line of the Isaiah text, "and the day of vengeance of our God," which held hope for the defeat of all their enemies. Instead, Jesus spoke of God's mercy to the widow of Sidon and the leper of Syria. Hearing the preaching of Christ brought about a crisis of faith.

St. Paul's mission order distills the long history of hearing God's word and makes it central in the church's mission order. The hearing that makes faith possible is the hearing that also brings about a crisis of faith between the claims and promises of God in Christ on the one hand and all competing claims and promises on the other.

But does that mission order apply to North American churches that have pews? Is hearing "the word of faith," as St. Paul put it, central to the mission of established churches as most North American Christians know them? Or is hearing God's message only central to "missions" somewhere out there among other people who have not yet heard?

Let us consider the case of St. John's on the Corner, a typical, well-established church in North America. St. John's happens to be Lutheran, but denominational identity is not relevant for our question. Is hearing central to the mission of St. John's on the Corner?

Last Sunday Pastor Olsen read the fourth chapter of the Gospel according to Luke before he preached the sermon. The lesson reported how Jesus entered the synagogue in his hometown on the sabbath, read part of Isaiah 61 from the scroll, and handed the scroll back to the attendant. All eyes were fixed on Pastor Olsen as he announced that the text for the sermon was the sermon of Jesus: "Today this scripture has been fulfilled in your hearing."

The nine-word sermon became an eighteen-minute sermon. He explained how the exiles first heard the words of Jesus' text, how the people in the synagogue heard Jesus' sermon, how Theophilus (the Greek Christian to whom Luke wrote his Gospel first) heard his report, and how they could hear the Good News of Jesus Christ in the lesson for today. It was a good sermon. The people at St. John's heard the Good News of what God had done for them in Jesus Christ and were challenged not to allow even inherited religious traditions to get in the way of living and dying by that News.

But is listening to sermons the center of St. John's mission? Is the pew central in what God calls them to be and do?

It may appear to some of the members that sending missionaries is central to their mission. The church has done so for many years, and pictures of their missionaries are displayed in the library. It seems to some of the members that calling on the name of the Lord should be central to what they are about. That fits with their frequent calls to prayer and with their Wednesday prayer services. Most of the members, if polled, would vaguely regard listening to sermons as somehow self-serving. Hiring a preacher falls into the category of "business expenses," the cost of staying afloat. How, then, does St. John's fit St. Paul's mission order, given that last Sunday Pastor Olsen spent eighteen minutes explaining Jesus' nine-word sermon, and one-third of the church's budget goes toward paying his salary?

St. John's has been on the corner for ninety-eight years. During that time, Sidney Ericson would tell you, they have "gone through twelve pastors and are on their thirteenth." It did not begin because some missionaries were sent there to preach, and when people heard, they believed and called upon the name of the Lord. Rather, it was started by Lutheran immigrants from Norway who did not feel at home in other churches. They believed the gospel of Jesus and called upon the name of the Lord even before they arrived in the New World. What they needed was a church where they could hear the word of God, practice their faith, and call on the name of the Lord in ways they knew best.

So they called pastors throughout the years. While they prayed that God would *send* them a pastor, they had long meetings to sort through information about candidates, establish salary and benefit allowances, and court the acceptance of the pastor of their choice. No one *sent* them a pastor the way they sent missionaries to Chile; they hired one who came to them from another state.

How does St. Paul's mission order fit what happens at St. John's? Can listening to sermons stand at the center of their mission? Yes it can.

There is an important sense in which calling a pastor to preach entails sending a pastor. After all, the "sending" mentioned in St. Paul's mission order is not a matter of giving someone a trip but of giving someone a *task*. When St. John's installed a pastor for its pulpit, they were sending

that pastor as fully as when they sent a missionary to Chile.
Each time they installed a pastor, the members were ad-
mitting something about themselves: they needed to hear
the Word of God. In words their Lutheran parents had
taught them, they acknowledged that they were sinners
made righteous in Christ alone. They celebrated their peace
with God but knew they were not yet renewed in God's
image or fully restored to his service. Though their salvation was complete in Christ, they knew it was not complete
in themselves, that they needed to go on hearing the message that nurtures trust, deepens love, and brightens hope.
They understood the apostle Peter's confession that *he*
needed yet to be saved when he said to his enemies, "there
is no other name under heaven given among men by which
we must be saved" (Acts 4:12). St. Paul's mission order
does fit the mission at St. John's. A church that is born
through hearing "the word of faith" lives and serves by
continuing to hear that word.

The hearing that was central to the church's mission
was threatened from the beginning. The threats began in
Jerusalem, where the authorities demanded that the apostles stop speaking in the name of Jesus. Peter and John
responded with a powerful helplessness: "we cannot but
speak of what we have seen and heard" (Acts 4:20). And
they prayed for boldness to keep speaking so others could
hear (Acts 4:29). Danger soon came from the Roman Em-
pire, which was threatened when believers confessed Jesus
Christ as Lord (Acts 17:6-7). For more than three centuries,
persecution threatened to quench the hearing of the word
of faith.

But when prosperity and privilege gave the church a
different kind of power in the world, the church itself
became hard of hearing. In the sixteenth century Martin

Luther strained mightily to hear, but the voices he heard deepened his despair. Still, there was a voice to be heard, a word of faith to break the silence, and Luther heard, believed, and called upon the name of the Lord.

It is no wonder that when Martin Luther and John Calvin spoke about how God works to save people, they both said: through *preaching!* It is the preaching of the word, they said, that brings faith to people and people to faith. Against the abuses of the hard-of-hearing church that had silenced the Good News, they proclaimed that preaching is the means by which God brings salvation in Christ to people.

But the Reformers assumed that when preaching happened, hearing would happen. They assumed that most — if not all — hearing would take place because of preaching. But in their new emphasis on preaching in an effort to correct church deafness and corruption, they may unintentionally have had the effect of removing *hearing* from its central place in St. Paul's mission order.

When John Calvin commented on Romans 10:17 ("Faith comes from hearing, and hearing through the preaching of Christ"), he wrote about preaching but not about hearing. He exalted the human voice as a marvelous instrument of God but said nothing about the ear. In his commentary on this text, he wrote that "this is a remarkable passage with regard to the efficacy of preaching; for he testifies, that by it faith is produced." But Calvin did not intend thereby to remove hearing from its central place. Indeed, when he set forth the marks of the church he began by saying, "wherever we see the Word of God purely preached *and heard* . . ." (*Institutes,* 4.1.9).

A subtle shift takes place when children of the Reformation allow the Reformers' emphasis on preaching to displace St. Paul's "faith comes from hearing" with "faith comes from preaching." This shift from hearing to preaching may seem insignificant, but in fact it can change the character of the church, change the way we view what happens in Christian worship. Compare these two ways of seeing worship at St. John's:

Preaching is Central	Hearing is Central
1. The preacher is the focus of the action.	1. The congregation is the focus of the action.
2. The congregation comes for the sermon.	2. The sermon comes for the congregation.
3. The minister speaks the sermon and listens for response.	3. The minister listens and speaks a response in the sermon.
4. The minister finishes the sermon.	4. The congregation finishes the sermon.
5. The test of value lies in what is said.	5. The test of value lies in what is heard.

If hearing the word of faith is central to the church's mission order, then listening for the word of faith is central to the church's responsibility. Listening is a task that engages the congregation with the preacher. We work at hearing by listening. It is, of course, possible to hear without listening, as when we hear a neighbor's radio playing while focusing on a conversation with a friend. And it is also possible to listen without hearing, as when we listen to an unfamiliar language or get a bad connection on the phone: we strain to comprehend but fail to understand. But if hearing the word of God is the purpose of preaching and the means by which we come to believe, then we in the pew have a responsibility to make an effort to listen in order that we might hear.

The church must be a sending community, a preaching community, a believing community, and a community that calls on the name of the Lord. If we fail to be a hearing community as well, the whole order collapses. What remains may be a religious society that preserves tradition and promotes good causes, but it will not be the church of the crucified and risen Lord.

It has been common among Christians especially in the past twenty years to lament the condition of the church. One line of complaint is that the church feeds itself with word and sacrament but never does anything. Members receive but do not give. The complaint usually results in a resolution that it is time to cut down on the church's diet and begin a vigorous exercise program.

But before rushing in to reprogram the church for action, it is wise to check what the members have actually been *hearing*. That requires some comparing of what was said with what was heard. After a recent sermon in which the preacher vigorously challenged the church to evangelism, one member responded by saying that it is too bad that the preacher did not have time to do what he loved best. That is what he heard. David Buttrick has observed that

> most preachers have been appalled by the way in which sermons can be heard. A minister may get up and with wondrous glee announce the free gracious mercy of God, only to have some parishioner come up after the sermon and say something like, "That's right, preacher, unless we repent, God won't forgive us!" The preacher is left reeling in confusion, wondering what on earth went wrong with the sermon. Too easily we blame listeners.[2]

2. Buttrick, *Homiletic: Moves and Structures* (Philadelphia: Fortress Press, 1987), p. 30.

When the preaching and listening work together so that *hearing* happens, the diet may improve and the exercise program may not be necessary.

Faith comes from what is heard. That is why St. Paul's mission order includes a church order and a salvation order: Sending — Preaching — *Hearing* — Believing — Calling on the name of the Lord. That order has survived waves of persecution and prosperity alike. But when children of the Reformation shift the center of the church's mission order from *hearing* to *preaching,* we miss Calvin and Luther's intent and leave some Reformation business unfinished.

If faith comes from hearing, then the pew is still central to the church's mission. When we listen to sermons, *we have the right to sit at the center of the church's mission.*

— 2 —

A Pioneer Listener

A PIONEER is a person who goes on ahead of a group of travelers to make it safe for them to follow. The pioneer scouts ahead, explores, examines, risks, discovers, and suffers if necessary, on behalf of fellow travelers who will take the same path.

According to Hebrews 2:10, Jesus is the pioneer of our salvation. And this is how he pioneered to make it safe for us to follow: "since therefore children share in flesh and blood, he himself likewise partook of the same nature, that through death he might destroy him who has the power of death, that is, the devil, and deliver all those who through fear of death were subject to lifelong bondage" (Heb. 2:14-15).

When we listen to sermons, we are the fellow travelers. Life is a flesh-and-blood journey through death that has been pioneered for us by Jesus. He has made it safe for us to follow and has delivered us from the paralyzing fear of the journey. Along the way, we listen to those who have pioneered for us in other ways. When we listen to sermons, *we have the right to hear a pioneer listener speak.*

If hearing the preaching of Christ stands at the center of the church's mission, then listening is central to the church's task. But how can the church hear? By appointing pioneer listeners who can help us hear along the journey. Pews represent the place where we listen and hear, but we should not think of them as being nailed down. They accompany us on the journey. They are vehicles of a sort. When we sit in them, we hear our pioneer listeners speak the word of faith for the journey.

Preachers are pioneer listeners on behalf of the community of faith. Preachers who remain behind the travelers to take pictures and keep records of what happened along the way cannot help us with what is ahead. Preachers who remain in the company of the faithful without risking the look ahead and around may be able to help us with what's happening now but they will not be able to lead us safely around the bend. Preachers should be listeners before they are speakers.

When a person is ordained to the ministry of the Word and sacraments in the church I serve, the liturgy and vows give no indication that the preacher is called to be a pioneer listener. When we ask "what the Scriptures say concerning the office of the minister of the Word," we are told that the minister is called to four tasks: (1) to preach the gospel of the kingdom, (2) to administer the sacraments that the Lord has instituted as signs and seals of his grace, (3) to pray steadfastly for the whole family of God, and (4) to shepherd the people of God in the Christian life. Following this explanation, the minister is asked to declare that he believes God has called him to this ministry and he believes the Holy Scriptures to be the Word of God. Then he is asked to make the ordination promises: "Do you promise to discharge the duties of your office faithfully, to conduct yourself worthily of this calling, and to submit yourself to the government and discipline of the church?"

Where in this ordination ritual is the minister commissioned to be a pioneer listener on behalf of the church and world? No doubt that task is simply assumed under the first assignment: to preach the gospel of the kingdom. Just as children of the Reformation tend to shift from St. Paul's "faith comes from hearing" to "faith comes from preaching," something similiar has happened here. If we assume that listening is included in the preaching task, we feel no need to take note of listening before speaking. But that assumption leaves hidden what needs to be brought into the open between pew and pulpit — namely, that preachers are pioneer listeners on behalf of the community of faith.

Peter had to learn to listen before speaking. He is exposed in the Gospels as a disciple whose speaking Jesus frequently rebuked. The experience on the mount of transfiguration was stunning in its beauty and uniqueness for Peter. The three of them — Peter, James, and John — saw Jesus' glory unveiled before their eyes as he spoke with Moses and Elijah. Peter loved the experience and wanted to make it permanent. He offered to make three booths, one each for Jesus, Moses, and Elijah. But while Peter was *still speaking,* a voice from the cloud said, "This is my beloved Son . . . *listen to him*" (Matt. 17:5).

The Gospel of Mark introduces what many have called the Parable of the Sower with a command from Jesus: "Listen" (Mark 4:3). And in spite of other differences, Matthew, Mark, and Luke all conclude the parable with the same words: "He who has ears, let him hear."

A veteran teacher of preachers, Merrill Abbey, tells us about the importance of listening before speaking:

before we are *interpreters* of the Word, we are sinful men
who stand in desperate need to *hear* it. On our hearing
hangs our own salvation. But we are charged with the
pastoral care of God's people, and our hearing of their need
is crucial to that ministry. Nor can we *interpret* a Word we
have not first attentively heard; it is our occupational
hazard that we are speaking men and may be so driven by
the question, "What shall I say?" that we find little time
to ask, "What is God saying?"[1]

And James Daane, whose understanding of preaching is
controlled completely by the message of the text, emphasizes
the importance of listening to the text before preaching:

There is another subtle temptation to be avoided. The
primary concern with which preachers often approach a
text is a concern for "what it means for the hearer today."
Eager to discover relevance, the minister never takes time
to hear what the text really says. The desire to apply it
takes precedence over hearing what it declares. Application
dominates interpretation. Students are particularly prone
to this folly — and folly it is, for how can one apply what
one has not yet heard or understood?[2]

Preparation for each sermon requires a careful listening to the Bible text. The church through its seminaries
prepares students to practice the art of listening to texts in
disciplined ways. Tools are provided and skills are developed to enable the preacher to listen before speaking. Good

---

1. Abbey, *The Word Interprets Us* (Nashville: Abingdon Press,
1967), p. 64; italics his.
2. Daane, *Preaching with Confidence: A Theological Essay on
the Power of the Pulpit* (Grand Rapids: William B. Eerdmans, 1980),
p. 61.

listening to a Bible text requires that the preacher knows what kind of questions to ask, what clues to meaning to look for, how to learn from comparing text with text, and how to distinguish and then bring back together the questions "What did the text mean for those who first heard?" and "What does the text mean for us now?" Listening to a text in order to speak from it requires that we carry on a discussion and even a debate with the text. Preparing to preach requires that the preacher wrestle with the text and not let it go until it yields a blessing worth bringing to the pew.

There are many obstacles to that kind of listening today. Besides the built-in obstacle of listening to a Bible text across the distance of centuries, the barriers of language, and the chasm of different cultures, there are two other obstacles to the kind of listening preaching requires: the church's expectations of the pastor and the pastor's familiarity with the Bible text.

Listening time is precious for the preacher these days not only because it is valuable but also because it is scarce. Using the terms of the Parable of the Sower, we might say that the preacher's life bears enough traffic to harden a well-worn path right where the seed is needed most. The preacher shares that burden with the listening community of faith. The traffic of news, events, demands, and cares compels the preacher to experience in the privacy of the study what the listeners experience when they come to the pew. As a pioneer listener, the preacher can identify with the listening community of faith. The freedom to listen so that we can hear, believe, and call upon the name of the Lord must be protected against the odds.

But assuming the preacher can hurdle this first obstacle to listening to the Bible text, the second still remains: famil-

iarity. The text for next Sunday is the parable of the Good
Samaritan or the story of Moses at the burning bush or the
story of David and Goliath or the miracle of healing the ten
lepers. We know these stories. They are as familiar as an old
pair of shoes. So the preacher rushes to find ways to apply
them creatively and to make them interesting. Or she moves
from the text to a church doctrine suggested by the story and
then looks for illustrations or applications that will make the
doctrine more attractive this time around. Instead of careful
listening to the Bible text, the preacher searches for ways to
make familiar teachings interesting.

The minister, however, is not called first of all to be
creative; he or she is called to be a faithful listener so that
others can hear the Word of God. Listening patiently and
attentively to a Bible text, using available tools and skills,
the pioneer listener can cut through the crust of familiarity
and taste the bread of life afresh before breaking it for
others.

As a member of the listening, journeying community,
the minister listens in the place and on behalf of others.
He brings the eyes and ears and lives of the community
with him to the act of listening to the text. Thomas Long
has noted that

> some preachers find it helpful, as part of the process of
> interpreting the scripture, to visualize the congregation that
> will be present when the sermon is preached. They survey
> the congregation in their mind's eye, seeing there the fa-
> miliar faces and the lives behind them. They see the adults
> and the children, the families and those who are single,
> those who participate actively in the church's mission and
> those who stand cautiously on the edges of the church's
> life. They see those for whom life is full and good and
> those for whom life is composed of jagged pieces. They see

the regulars sitting in their customary places, and they see the stranger, the newcomer, the visitor, hesitating and wondering if there is a place for them. They see the people who are there, and they see the people who cannot be there, or who choose not to be there. When preachers turn to the scripture, all these people go with them.[3]

Seeing the minister as a pioneer listener on behalf of the community of faith is, in part at least, an answer to a recurring question in the church: What is the relationship between preacher and congregation, or "clergy and laity"? At the extremes, some preachers have said, "Just call me Joe; I'm no different than you," while others have said, "I'm the authority around here who dispenses God's grace and truth." But if the preacher is a pioneer listener, he or she is both identified with and distinguished within the community of faith. The preacher shares membership in the human family and the body of Christ but is commissioned to a task on their behalf.

Pioneer listeners need to listen *to* the congregation and *with* the congregation in order to listen *for* the congregation. Only then will they be able to speak *to, with, and for* them with grace and truth. As a pioneer listener, the minister will need to go on ahead to listen in advance, but she will take care not to get out of the range of the congregation's hearing. She will listen to the scriptures within range of their voices so that when the sermon is preached, they will be within range of hers.

Frederick Buechner has seen that hearing the truth in order to tell the truth requires that the preacher experience

---

3. Long, *The Witness of Preaching* (Louisville: Westminster/John Knox, 1989), p. 56.

this identity with the congregation: "the preacher must always try to feel what it is like to live inside the skins of the people he is preaching to, to hear the truth as they hear it. That is not as hard as it sounds because, of course, he is himself a hearer of truth as well as a teller of truth, and he listens out of the same emptiness as they do for a truth to fill him and make him true."[4]

Another teacher is persuaded that preachers and listeners can be so united in their life concerns that the preachers can preach to their own needs and thereby address the needs of others. Listening to, with, and for the listening community must be intimate in order to risk following the advice of J. Randall Nichols: "we must add another piece of advice to students and ministers: *preach to and for yourselves*. If you as pastors are truly living the lives of your people, if you are tuning into their own situations and making them your own, then you should trust that what concerns you as their pastor is also their concern. Preach to that."[5]

This kind of listening to, with, and for people is similar to praying. Leander E. Keck sees a clear parallel between the minister's priestly acts of listening and praying: "the preacher listens for a word not only as a private citizen but as a representative of the church. The preacher's listening and hearing is a priestly act. Because praying for people is a priestly act we understand, it is useful to compare this kind of praying with listening/hearing."[6] In the ordination

4. Buechner, *Telling the Truth: The Gospel as Tragedy, Comedy, and Fairy Tale* (New York: Harper & Row, 1977), p. 8.

5. Nichols, *Building the Word: The Dynamics of Communication and Preaching* (New York: Harper & Row, 1980), p. 40.

6. Keck, *The Bible in the Pulpit* (Nashville: Abingdon Press, 1978), p. 61.

liturgy I cited earlier, preaching and praying are tasks assigned to the minister. These are usually distinguished as prophetic (preaching) and priestly (praying). It may be helpful to note that listening to, with, and for the people is essential for both prophets and priests.

If we understand the preacher's task as that of a pioneer listener whose priestly listening is similar to priestly praying, we may be able to understand better some other concerns of church members. An exchange took place on the subject of preaching some years ago between Nicholas Wolterstorff and Richard Mouw in *The Reformed Journal* that raised some important issues. The discussion began when Mouw wondered how we can explain the existence of bad sermons if we believe that sermons are the very Word of God. He described the problem, and offered a possible solution:

> My problem with the high view [of preaching] is this: How, if we accept it, do we explain bad sermons? This view seems to me to picture the situation as involving a divide, with the congregation on one side and God and the minister on the other. But the picture doesn't seem to hold up when, try as we might, we can't hear in the minister's words anything that sounds as if it is coming from the other side of the divide.
>
> What would be wrong with this alternative picture: The divide is there, and God is on one side. We, the congregation, along with the minister, are on the other side; but the minister is standing out a little bit in front of the rest, peering across the divide, equipped perhaps with special glasses which the rest of us lack. Then, when what he says to us (over his shoulder, as it were) does not sound like an accurate description of what is across the divide, we can rightly conclude that he failed to get far enough

ahead of us, or he hadn't cleaned his lenses, or he had something in his eye.[7]

From there, Wolterstorff and Mouw carried on correspondence that resulted in their reaching some agreement on how we can believe that God speaks through preaching and still not be inconsistent or guilty if we say that a given sermon is bad. Hearing bad sermons should not tempt us to give up the view that God can speak through preaching any more than bad parents should tempt us to give up the view that God works through parenting. Wolterstorff and Mouw also agreed that God speaks to his people in a unique way through preaching. Unlike casual conversations in which people talk about God or their faith, preaching takes place in the context of the church's discipline, and this has significant implications for the character of what is said.

"I hold," wrote Wolterstorff, "that by way of the preacher speaking, God may speak. Therein lies the 'highness' of sermons, though not indeed their uniqueness. Their (relative) uniqueness consists in the fact that we characteristically must take them with more seriousness, as bearers of God's Word, than we must most other situations, and that because of the context of discipline around them."[8] This view of preaching does not guarantee that there will not be bad sermons, but neither does it require that we abandon a high view of preaching when we hear a bad one. "A bad sermon is nothing more nor less than a sermon in which the minister not at all, or scarcely at

7. Mouw, "Bad Sermons," *Reformed Journal,* November 1976, p. 5.

8. Wolterstorff, "Are 'Bad Sermons' Possible? An Exchange on Preaching," *Reformed Journal,* November 1977, p. 11.

all, speaks on God's behalf, or in which he does so only in a vague and muffled manner."[9]

Mouw's misfortune in having heard some bad sermons opened up a very helpful discussion that should be revived now and again. It was unfortunate, however, that his first attempt to answer his own problem was left behind in the discussion that followed. His picture of a minister standing with the congregation on one side of the divide, moving on ahead with special glasses to see what he can see, and then speaking over his shoulder to the rest of us to let us know what he sees is a realistic view of preaching. Nor does it stand against the conclusions that Mouw and Wolterstorff seem to have reached about sermons. Mouw's image of the minister as a pioneer *seer* has to do with the *listening* side of the preaching task. Their discussion shifted too soon to the *speaking* side of the preaching task. The quality of the listening is directly related to the quality of the speaking.

Thomas Long has offered a parable that changes and expands Mouw's analogy:

> Imagine that the biblical text for next Sunday's sermon is not a piece of literature but a deep and mysterious cave. The preacher is a trained explorer of caves who descends into this one, flashlight and ropes in hand, filled with the excitement of discovery. Others have explored this cave before, indeed the preacher has read their accounts, studied their maps, been excited by the sights they have seen, marveled at the treasures they have discovered, and is impelled by their assurances that there are new treasures yet to be found. The preacher moves ever deeper into the cave, sometimes ambling easily through wide passageways,

9. Wolterstorff, "Are 'Bad Sermons' Possible?" p. 9.

other times wedging his way through an opening barely large enough to squeeze through. He wanders down alluring grottos, only to find they end in cold, blank walls. He shines his light across chasms too wide for him to cross with the equipment he has. He inches his way down a high and narrow ledge, once almost losing his footing and tumbling into the black infinity below. Suddenly, he turns a corner and there it is, what he has been looking for all along. Perhaps it is a waterfall, tumbling from a great height to the floor below. Or perhaps it is an enormous stalactite, an icicle eons old which overwhelms him by its sheer size. Or maybe his flashlight has illumined a wall of gems, filling the dark space with dancing fire and color. He stands before the sight in a moment of awe and silence. Then, knowing what he must do, he carefully retraces his path, scrambles to the mouth of the cave, and with the dirt of the journey still on his face and his flashlight waving excitedly, he calls to those who have been waiting on him, "Come on, Have I got something to show you!"[10]

Long's parable captures the spirit of adventure, risk, and discovery that can bring a pioneer listener to stand before the people on whose behalf he has explored. Being where we are on our journey, the suspense of waiting for the Word is a good way to hear the suspense in such words as these: "The kingdom of heaven is like . . ."

For those who prefer severe obedience to joyful discovery, Jeremiah's word about false prophets who speak without listening will do: "For who among them has stood in the council of the LORD to perceive and to hear his word, or who has given heed to his word and listened?" (Jer. 23:18).

10. Long, "The Distance We Have Traveled: Changing Trends in Preaching," *Reformed Liturgy and Music* 17 (Winter 1983): 14.

Those who preach need to listen before they speak, to see before they say. Listening to, with, and for the listening community of faith will bring the preacher to the text ready to hear. Listening for that Word with priestly compassion will prepare the preacher to speak also with prophetic power.

Whoever has ears, let him hear: *When we listen to sermons, we have the right to hear a pioneer listener speak.*

— 3 —

Hiding among the Trees

THE FIRST SERMON was heard by people who were hiding among the trees. They heard the voice of God calling, "Where are you?" (Gen. 3:9).

We listen to sermons while sitting on padded pews cut from oak trees, on steel chairs that fold for storage, on fiberglass chairs contoured for comfort. We are not hiding. We are there to listen and hear. We even call on the name of the Lord *before* the sermon comes when we say, "Speak, Lord, for your servants are listening."

But we are also hiding among the trees. Let the trees of Eden stand for all of the needs we bring to the pew. Our needs bring us there — close enough to hear. But our needs also keep us at a safe distance. Like the trees of Eden, our needs make us bend our ears to hear, but they also distract us from hearing.

We may wish that listening to a sermon would be like leaving all of our needs behind and hearing the unobstructed voice of God clearly with unplugged ears in the wide open spaces of paradise. But we can listen for the voice of God only from within our needs, among the trees. The needs that draw us to listen are the same needs that plug our ears, distract our attention, and compete with the voice. When we listen to a sermon, we listen among the trees. We have no other place.

The good news is that God knows about trees and about hiding. When he spoke in the Garden, he pretended not to know where his people were or what was happening. But his Word penetrated their screen and coaxed them out of hiding. When their fear of hiding was greater than their fear of being found, his voice won and they were ready to answer.

When we listen to sermons, *we have the right to hear a Word addressed to our deepest needs.*

· When a sermon comes to us, we do not have our needs all neatly packaged so that we can open them and have them met one by one as we listen. We come with a confusion of needs — needs we want to hide, needs that cry out to be met, needs that can wait, and needs we do not even know. We need to be addressed in our needs, and we cannot even understand them without the grace that brings the remedy. Adam and Eve thought they were just hiding, but when the Voice came with the searching question "Where are you?" they knew the truth: they were lost.

The needs we carry to the pew are not separate from the ordinary concerns and routines of life. They are tied up with specific people, debts, cars, children, neighbors, plumbing, and jobs. We come to worship carrying whatever settles down within us from all that goes on around us. On any Sunday morning people gather in churches to give thanks for a birthday, to sigh with relief for having made it through another week, to confess sins, to mourn the loss of a job or friend, to wonder whether nuclear bombs threaten us more than they protect us, to find wisdom and courage to save a fragile marriage, to tame a rebellious child, to get help to love a miserable neighbor. Our needs are tied up with the stuff of daily life. The Word of God that reached through the trees to Adam and Eve reached again last Sunday to their children while they sat in the pews.

Lewis Smedes looks at the church on Sunday morning and sees that

> a man and woman, sitting board-straight, smiling on cue at every piece of funny piety, are hating each other for letting romance in their marriage collapse on a tiring treadmill of tasteless, but always tidy, tedium.
>
> A widow, whispering her Amens to every promise of divine providence, is frightened to death because the unkillable beast of inflation is devouring her savings.
>
> A father, the congregational model of parental firmness, is fuming in the suspicion of his own fatherly failure because he cannot stomach, much less understand, the furious antics of his slightly crazy son.
>
> An attractive young woman in the front pew is absolutely paralyzed, sure she has breast cancer.
>
> A middle-aged fellow who, with his new Mercedes, is an obvious Christian success story, is wondering when he will ever have the guts to tell his boss to take his lousy job and shove it.
>
> A submissive wife of one of the elders is terrified because she is being pushed to face up to her closet alcoholism.
>
> Ordinary people, all of them, and there are a lot more where they came from.[1]

William D. Thompson cares about biblical preaching because he knows the needs of people.

1. Smedes, "Preaching to Ordinary People," *Leadership* 4 (Fall 1983): 116.

Certainly the congregation cares that the preaching it hears be biblical. For one thing, its members want and need to be constantly hearing the good news that God was in Christ, reconciling *their* world to himself. To church every Sunday come parents of troubled teen-agers, adults whose singleness is a crushing load, young people suffocating in a depersonalized high school, grandparents forgotten and unappreciated, children eager for approval. For a time they can endure sermons of good advice, autobiographical revelations, discussions of interesting theological topics, commentaries on the social issues of the day, even explanations of biblical texts. But it was not with such preaching that the church was built, and it is not through such preaching that it will be saved.[2]

But what are the needs that come with us to the pew? How shall we identify them so that we will know when the Word has reached us where we are?

There are two ways we can try to identify the needs within which we listen for the Word of God. One way is to examine our needs with the help of skilled observers, classify them, give them priority, and then bring them with us when we listen to a sermon. Some people have taken this path on their spiritual journeys. Knowing their needs, they listened until a message came that lifted the burden, transformed the need, or simply gave them the grace to live with it in creative ways. Had Adam and Eve hiding in the garden taken this path, they might have examined their situation and needs. They had lost their freedom, their play, their work, their relationship. They were cut off from their past and could not find the door to the future. They were

2. Thompson, *Preaching Biblically* (Nashville: Abingdon Press, 1981), p. 12.

afraid. Finding more creative ways to hide would not be the answer. Within those needs, the voice of God came: "Where are you?" And this Word reached through all of their needs and found them.

So the first path we might take is to come from our needs to the voice. The other path involves coming from the voice to the needs, listening to the voice of God and seeing our needs in its light. When God asked "Where are you?" in the Garden, the question cast a light that exposed Adam and Eve's needs starkly: they were lost. What they experienced as hiding turned out to be something different. They were lost from God and therefore they suffered all the losses of freedom, work, play, each other, a meaningful past, a hopeful future, and all the rest. The voice of God that found them and saved them from hiding is the voice that identified and interpreted their deepest need: they were lost.

If we take the second path, moving from the voice to our place in the pew, what do our crying needs turn out to look like? To find out we must leave the garden and turn to the center of God's Story, where the voice of God became flesh and blood in Jesus of Nazareth. We can identify three moments in that Story that render it good news for all times and places: Jesus' birth, death, and resurrection. This is what happened to the voice of God in the garden: he was born in Bethlehem, he died on a cross outside Jerusalem, and on the third day his former friends found the grave empty and met him alive in familiar places. Those events are the center of God's Story and the heart of the good news.

In the light of these events and this news, what do our needs turn out to look like? If we move from this Word made flesh to where we are, what needs do we see?

I submit that the light of this Story exposes our need for dignity, meaning, and hope. In the light of Jesus' birth our need for dignity is addressed: he took our flesh and blood and accepted all the conditions of being human. In the light of Jesus' death our need for meaning in an absurd, senseless world is addressed: the day on which the worst thing that could happen *did* happen we now call *Good* Friday. In the light of Jesus' resurrection our need for hope is addressed: the empty tomb is the womb of the new creation. The deepest needs in which we are hiding and from which we listen to sermons are exposed by the Good News: we need dignity, meaning, and hope.

It is weakness that assaults our dignity, and everyone knows what it is like to be weak. Therapists know that when a person gets his or her identity from weaknesses to the exclusion of almost everything else, that person suffers the loss of self-esteem — or dignity. We experience weakness in an infinite variety of ways and combinations. We feel it when we find that we can't lift a box, when we can't answer a question, when we can't get over the flu, when we can't quiet a crying child, when we can't find a job, when we can't pass a course in school, when we can't understand what is happening, when we can't learn to trust God. We are weak in ways we know and do not yet know, in ways we dare to show and do not dare to show. Weakness assaults our dignity.

Mixed with weakness, we have strength. People do not come in two varieties: weak and strong. We are all strong and weak in different ways, and we experience our strength in as many different ways as we experience our weakness. We call someone's name and feel the power to command their attention — at least for a moment. Children learn the power of a cry for help when it draws a response. We have strength to build and break, learn and make music, raise crops and drive trucks, laugh and play, heal and hurt, wage war and make peace.

What is at stake in this mix of weakness and strength? Our dignity. If strength gives dignity and weakness robs us of it, then we can maintain our dignity only by flexing strength and denying weakness. And if weakness holds the final "power" over strength — as death whispers so hauntingly — then dignity must finally be an illusion and the quest for it futile. "Death with dignity" is a lie if death is the ultimate weakness and weakness destroys dignity.

The Word that became flesh in Jesus of Nazareth is the word that comes to us in the sermon. It is a Word about one who entered into our weakness. He was not born amid symbols of power. He was sheltered in a barn, wrapped in rags, hurried off to Egypt to escape the sword of Herod. In his ministry he gave signs of his power over demons, disease, and death, but his power was always wrapped in weakness. He was hungry, tired, thirsty. He wept, suffered, and died. His weakness offended his friends and amused his enemies at the cross. The Word we hear in a sermon that is spoken in the name of Jesus is a Word about dignity in the face of weakness. Jesus was no less God's Son in his weakness than in his strength. In his birth and life he accepted all the conditions of our humanness and made it possible for us to live and die — weakness and all — as children of God. A trusting relationship with him gives us a dignity that frees us to be weak without indignity and strong without arrogance. In fellowship with God's family in Christ, we receive a dignity that embraces us in life and in death.

We also bring with us to the pew the need for meaning in life. When life loses meaning, makes no sense, and becomes a nightmare, then it loses purpose. When meaning is gone, we become aimless — lost. Purpose in life depends on finding some meaning that will stay in place.

What assaults meaning in life? Let's call it chaos. It is chaos like the primal slime, "without form and void," from which God ordered the creation (Gen. 1:2). Chaos continues to haunt life in God's ordered — but fallen — world. Sometimes it erupts on a large scale that defies finding meaning, as in the holocaust or in the mass suicides commanded by the Rev. Jim Jones in Guyana. More often the chaos is contained in smaller but no less senseless situations, as in an earthquake in San Francisco when a World Series baseball game is about to begin. Order preserves meaning in life; chaos empties it of meaning. When we listen to a sermon, we bring with us the experience of chaos and order in search for meaning.

Order is present when the house is cleaned, the pizza is ordered, and the guests are arriving. Chaos sets in when the party turns into a drunken bash. Order is present when everyone is playing the game according to the rules; chaos erupts when the teams empty the benches and slug it out on the field. Order is present when the whole family is present for a Thanksgiving dinner; chaos sets in when two of them are killed in an accident on the way home.

No one escapes the experience of chaos threatening life's order — although some get by with less hurt than others. What is at stake is the meaning and purpose of life. If meaning is present only when we can maintain order, then we will fight for order at any cost — even at the cost of creating chaos for others. Some, overwhelmed by chaos, will decide that meaning and purpose in life are impossible, and abandon all hope of making sense out of life.

The Word that became flesh in Jesus of Nazareth is

heard in a sermon that is spoken in his name. This Jesus was *crucified!* And it was not a lynching by an angry street gang; it happened at the hands of the religious leaders and the best judicial system the world had to offer. His death on the cross was an absurdity that Peter could not tame and the church may not remove: "You denied the Holy and Righteous One, and asked for a murderer to be granted to you, and killed the Author of life" (Acts 3:14-15). The crucifixion of Jesus was the darkest hour of the world's chaos.

Is there any meaning in the chaos of the cross? We need to see the absurdity in it more fully before we will find meaning. He was crucified, the witnesses testified afterward, not in spite of his being the Word made flesh, the Christ of God, but *because* of who he was. They teased him to come down from the cross to show that he was the Christ; he showed what it meant to be the Christ by staying there. And a final absurdity before the meaning can come: the witnesses offered the forgiveness of sins to those who crucified him because he died *for* them.

Jesus' own words give meaning to the absurdity of his crucifixion: "the Son of man came . . . to give his life as a ransom for many" (Matt. 20:28); "and I, when I am lifted up from the earth, will draw all men to myself" (John 12:32). No chaos could overcome his saving purpose. He took the chaos of the world to himself and gave his life to reconcile the world to God. Or, as St. Paul said, he traded his righteousness for our sin (2 Cor. 5:21).

When we listen to a sermon that is spoken in the name of this Crucified One, we bring our experience of chaos and order and listen for meaning in life. We cannot expect sermons to dispel all absurdity from life or to transform every experience of chaos into good order. That cannot happen as long as the crucifixion stands at the heart of God's Story. But we can expect to hear the Story: God was at work in the chaos of the cross to save those who hung Jesus there. It does not mean that his love can make us immune to chaos and absurdity, but neither can chaos or absurdity make us immune to his love. Perhaps both chaos and order in life are meant to point us to the question of how we can show what this God in Christ is like here and now.

We listen to sermons needing dignity, meaning, and hope in life. If weakness assaults dignity and chaos assaults meaning, it is danger that assaults hope. Life is dangerous. It is a terminal condition. We cannot live without hope.

From the beginning of life danger and safety touch us deeply. Who knows how deeply we feel the threat of danger and the comfort of safety in infancy, long before we have the words to name them? Danger comes when we are hungry, safety when we are fed. Danger comes when we are sick, safety when we recover. Danger is there when everyone is unfamiliar, safety when we are back home. Danger threatens when we are asked for more than we can give, safety when our needs are supplied. Danger and safety belong to human life in a multitude of patterns that are beyond tracing.

Do we live in a safe world that has its passing dangers? Or do we live in a dangerous world that has its passing moments of safety? What kind of world is this? Will safety or danger decide our destiny?

The Bible represents danger and safety in the symbols of two trees. After Adam and Eve were driven from the garden, God guarded the way to the tree of life with a flaming sword (Gen. 3:24). The sword and the tree of life represented danger.

But at the end of the Bible we are shown another tree
of life:

> Then he showed me the river of the water of life, bright
> as crystal, flowing from the throne of God and of the Lamb
> through the middle of the street of the city; also, on either
> side of the river, the tree of life with its twelve kinds of
> fruit, yielding its fruit each month; and the leaves of the
> tree were for the healing of the nations. (Rev. 22:1-2)

The two trees represent our life. Danger and safety, threat
and promise are both present. The Bible interprets our
life.

> These two biblical symbols, of threat and of promise, seem
> to open up one important possibility for our understanding
> of human existence, of life, and how one ought to live it.
> It is possible to argue that the Bible is dominated by pre-
> cisely these two symbols. It is concerned with the threat,
> and how the threat might be overcome, and every bit as
> much it is concerned with the promise, and how the prom-
> ise is fulfilled. And it is hardly accidental that these two
> symbols stand at the beginning and at the end of the Bible.
> In terms of the strategy of the biblical story they also stand
> at the beginning and end of time. At the end of the story,
> threat is swallowed up in promise and death gives way to
> life.[3]

All of us experience threat and promise, danger and
safety. But which is ultimate? If threat and danger are the
last words, then we have no hope. We come listening to
sermons — wondering.

3. George G. Nicol, "The Threat and the Promise," *Expository
Times* 94 (Feb. 1983): 136.

The sermon to which we listen is spoken in the name of the risen Christ. He overcame the threats of sin, death, and hell and carried his victory to the place where there are no more defeats. The world is not safe as the world regards safety: life is always terminal. And indeed, following the crucified, risen Christ may make it just that much more dangerous. But hope is not based on counting how many threats get carried out and how many promises get fulfilled. Christian hope is based on the resurrection of Jesus Christ. Peter's record as a disciple gives him the credentials needed to speak of hope: "Blessed be the God and Father of our Lord Jesus Christ! By his great mercy we have been born anew to a living hope through the resurrection of Jesus Christ from the dead" (1 Pet. 1:3).

Danger and safety, threat and promise are woven through our lives. Which is final? And how shall we know? When we listen to sermons preached in the name of the risen Christ, we hear the Story: the resurrection of Christ has made this world a safe place to die.

Genesis 3 shows us Adam and Eve hiding among the trees. That is where they heard the first sermon: "Where are you?" But we cannot know the depth of their need until we recognize that the sermon exposed the fact that they were lost. Similarly, we cannot read the clues to our own deepest needs until we recognize that God's Story has its center in the birth, death, and resurrection of Jesus. This enables us to comprehend the needs we bring to listening to sermons — the need for dignity, meaning, and hope.

The Word dawns on some gradually, others suddenly. But when we listen to sermons, *we have the right to hear a Word addressed to our basic human needs*. Listen to "The Sermon":

Adam, where are you?
Why hide
behind the tree
that sucks life
from fresh earth,
soaks light
between the nights,
and shimmers with my glory?

Adam, where are you?
Can trees betray
their gardener,
sheltering his prey?
Can trunks stay
my feet,
limbs my arms,
leaves my voice?

Adam, where are you?
How long must I pretend
not to know,
that you may know
and not pretend?
How long must my ear
await my voice
echo from your heart?

Adam, where are you?
Will you saw and sweat
to make a hiding place
of panelled palaces,
lacquered lecterns,
padded pews, or
satin stocks that shudder
at trigger's touch?

Adam, where are you?
Who forged the fear
that chains you
to the tree?
Your aprons weigh
like anchors
and the garden
wastes away.

Adam, where are you?
Shall I stab space
with lightning,
fill silence
with thunder,
strip forests bare
until there is
no hiding place?

Adam, where are you?
If I find your words,
will I find you?
My words are flesh,
my flesh is pressed
to branch bound branch
where no root comforts,
no leaf hides.

Adam, where are you?
You know the hell
of hiding;
I know the hell
of seeking;
calling, but none answers,
bleeding, but none heals,
waiting, but none comes.

Call my name, Adam.
I will be found.
Take my hand, Adam,
and work
the soil soft.
Watch my eye, Adam,
and we will see
new glory in the garden.

RVH, 1983

— PART II —

. . . From Bible Texts
in God's Story . . .

— 4 —

The Story behind the Text

"ONCE UPON A TIME . . ."

The words are like a spotlight that lights the stage before there are actors on it. They create expectation. They prepare us for a story and draw us into it.

Every sermon needs the spirit if not the letters of those words. Sermons are spoken from Bible texts, and God's Story lives behind those texts to give them their meaning and power and purpose. When we listen to sermons, *we have the right to see the Story behind the text.*

We *listen* to sermons to *see* the Story. Our ears and eyes work together when we listen. When we have heard the good news Story in a sermon, we can say, "I see! I see!"

Martin Luther warned that those who were not satisfied with hearing and wanted to see with their eyes were lost. He considered faith a matter of hearing. But for those who wanted to see, Luther had this advice: "Stick your eyes in your ears!"[1] Luther would agree that when

1. Luther, quoted by Richard Lischer in *A Theology of Preaching* (Nashville: Abingdon Press, 1981), p. 70.

we listen to a sermon, we have the right to see the Story behind the text.

This does not mean that when we listen to sermons we should expect to hear a string of stories — although sometimes we could do worse. It means that when we listen to a sermon we should be able to see the Story of what God has done for us in the history of Israel and in the person of Jesus Christ. Bible texts live in the Story that gave them birth, life, meaning, and purpose. When we listen to sermons, we should be able to see the drama, the good news Story of what God has done for us. That Story lives behind the Bible texts (some more visibly than others). If the Story shines in and through the text, it will also be visible in and through the sermon itself, and then in and through the lives of those who listen. The Story that gives meaning and purpose to the text gives meaning and purpose to the sermon and to the listeners who are drawn into it.

In a Christian doctrine class I teach for inquirers into the faith of the church, I note that I believe the gospel and I preach the gospel, and then I ask, "What is the gospel?" I watch the question work its way in and among the class members. They are thrown into a healthy state of confusion. Responses compete for prestige and piety: love, the Bible, the Word of God, the fact that there is a God, what we believe, how to be saved, the teachings of Jesus, what God wants us to do. After we have groped our way through the responses, someone timidly asks it as a question: The story?

Yes, *the Story.* The Story with a capital *S.* The gospel is the good news Story of what God has done for us in the history of Israel and in the person of Jesus Christ. The gospel is not a grand idea, a lofty ideal, a bit of good advice, a golden rule, or a worthy object. The gospel is *news* that can be announced, proclaimed, published, and heard. When we listen to sermons, we have a right to see the Story that lives behind, in, and through the text.

We can hear it in the ancient creed, which throbs with the Story: ". . . and in Jesus Christ, his only Son, our Lord, who was conceived by the Holy Spirit, born of the virgin Mary, suffered under Pontius Pilate, was crucified, died, and was buried. He descended into hell. The third day he arose. . . ." These words do not speak of good ideas or advice; they testify about persons and events in a Story.

People who have been taught by the Heidelberg Catechism are told about the Story. The teacher asks where we get this faith in Jesus Christ as the mediator between God and humankind. The student answers: "From the holy gospel, which God himself first revealed in Paradise; afterward published by the holy patriarchs and prophets, and foreshadowed by the sacrifices and other ceremonies of the law; and lastly fulfilled by His only begotten Son" (Answer 19). That is the language of story: "first revealed, . . . afterward published . . . foreshadowed, . . . and lastly fulfilled."

When we listen to sermons, we can expect to see the Story entitled "The Gospel of Jesus Christ."

The Story is named for its center in the birth, death, and resurrection of Jesus Christ. According to the Story, Jesus is the one God put forth to make peace between us and among us. Because of him, we can know that God is *for* us in spite of all else that we see and hear.

The Story reaches back to the beginning and forward to the new beginning. This Jesus is the fulfillment of all that came before him and is the promise of all that came after him. "Scripture teaches one universal kingdom history that encompasses all of created reality: past, present, and future," writes Sidney Greidanus. If that is true, then "every biblical passage must be understood in the context of this grand sweep of kingdom history."[2] And if that is true, then when we listen to sermons, the Story should show through the text.

William D. Thompson calls for perspective in speaking and listening to sermons: "the Bible is a witness to the saving activity of God in Jesus Christ, the meaning of whose life, death, and resurrection controls the meaning of every passage. How many messages can be preached from the Bible? What a silly question! On the surface of it, the answer is clear and obvious — hundreds, thousands, lifetimes. Perhaps. To look at the question another way, the answer is one — only one."[3]

The Story is behind the text and yet not only behind it: it also lives in and through the text. But it is important to recognize that it is behind the text, for this points us to the fact that it is the Story that gave birth and life to the text. God's people of the Old and New Testaments had the Story before they had the book. Sadly, there are sermons that rip the Bible text loose from the Story and treat it as though it gets its meaning from American history or as though it were just one more kind of good advice. Those who preach such sermons violate our pew rights.

Once upon a time I walked into an insurance office. The customer service counter offered me an array of business brochures and religious tracts while I waited. Looking

2. Greidanus, *The Modern Preacher and the Ancient Text* (Grand Rapids: William B. Eerdmans, 1988), pp. 95, 100.
3. Thompson, *Preaching Biblically* (Nashville: Abingdon Press, 1981), p. 74.

them over, I thought I saw a tract that had fallen into the business section by mistake. On closer examination, it turned out to be an insurance brochure with a Bible text printed on it: "The rain fell, and the floods came, and the winds blew and beat upon that house, but it did not fall, because it had been founded on the rock" (Matt. 7:25). Opening it, I was urged to purchase a certain kind of insurance protection so that if flood or wind came, my fortunes would not fall. When I saw the salesperson, I asked him if he saw how the brochure abused the Bible text. He said something like, "Well, yes, I suppose so. But this is a business, you know, not a church."

Business or church, I wondered how many sermons (including my own) detached the text from the Story so that it could serve alien purposes.

The sermon should help us see the Story that gave birth, life, meaning and purpose to the text. "Remember also your Creator in the days of your youth" (Eccles. 12:1) is not a bit of folk wisdom spoken by a midwestern farmer last year to restrain a teenage son. It is the voice of a wise man in Israel who, unable to make sense out of life, and fresh out of answers, bets his life on the rule and goodness of God anyway, trusting that God will vindicate his faith. St. Paul's instruction to remember the collection for the saints (1 Cor. 16:1) was not the appeal of a slick fund-raiser; it was the request of an apostle who had brought the good news Story from Jew to Gentile and now wanted to carry gifts from the Gentiles to the Jerusalem poor, thus displaying the power of the new family of God in Christ.

If the Story of what God has done for us in the history of Israel and in the person of Jesus Christ lies behind the Bible text, we have a right to see that story when we listen to sermons.

But that is where our problem with some Bible texts lies. Some texts seem to obscure the Story, or worse, tell an alien story. Bible texts — and sermons preached from them — do not all provide an equally transparent window on the Story. When we read Luke 2:14, the Story is right there, breathtaking and brilliant: "Glory to God in the highest, and on earth peace among men with whom he is pleased!" But what do we make of Jesus' words in the same Gospel of Luke: "Do you think I have come to give peace on earth? No, I tell you, but rather division" (12:51). Help! What happened to the Story?

We have no trouble seeing the Story in the great Advent lesson: "Comfort, comfort my people, says your God. Speak tenderly to Jerusalem, and cry to her that her warfare is ended, that her iniquity is pardoned, that she has received from the LORD's hand double for all her sins" (Isa. 40:1-2). But what do we hear or see in these words just eleven chapters earlier: "Stupefy yourselves and be in a stupor, blind yourselves and be blind! Be drunk, but not with wine; stagger, but not with strong drink! For the LORD has poured out upon you a spirit of deep sleep, and has closed your eyes, the prophets, and covered your heads, the seers" (Isa. 29:9-10)?

We see the Story quite clearly in Jesus' words: "the Son of Man came not to be served but to serve, and to give his life as a ransom for many" (Matt. 20:28). But can we see anything through his words just four chapters later: "wherever the body is, there the eagles will be gathered together" (24:28)?

Perhaps the Epistles will be consistently clear, letting us see the Story through every page. Try 1 Timothy: "the saying is sure and worthy of full acceptance, that Christ Jesus came into the world to save sinners. And I am the foremost of sinners; but I received mercy for this reason, that in me, as the foremost, Jesus Christ might display his perfect patience for an example to those who were to believe in him for eternal life. To the King of ages, immortal, invisible, the only God, be honor and glory for ever and ever. Amen" (1:15-17). Those words should be sung! But what happens to the Story two verses later: "By rejecting conscience, certain persons have made shipwreck of their faith, among them Hymenaeus and Alexander, whom I have delivered to Satan that they may learn not to blaspheme" (1:19-20). Who? What? Does Satan teach virtue? The Story seems eclipsed.

Some texts are transparent enough. When we hear sermons preached from them, the very least we want from the preacher is that he or she will not spoil them. Other texts seem to obscure the Story. When they are read, we call for help.

While I am writing these words, I am sitting at a desk next to a very large window overlooking a beautiful lake in Michigan. It is a grand September day and squeals of joy and laughter are coming from the lake. Twenty canoes are plying back and forth paddled by teenagers who are having the time of their lives. There is more to their story than I can see, but what I see in their play and laughter is a kind of doxology to the coming kingdom.

There is one slight problem. The window is smudged in places. The smudges call attention to themselves and get in the way of seeing the story on the lake. I need to clean the window so that it will not get in the way of my seeing the story out there.

When we sit in a pew and listen to Bible texts being read, it is like looking through a smudged window. We can see the Story, and it is breathtaking, but there are smudges that call attention to the text itself and get in the way of seeing the Story. As those who listen to sermons, we need preachers to clean the window so that we can see more clearly and fully. What we see of the Story excites us to want more. Perhaps we could even see the Story through Jesus' words about bringing division, not peace, or his talk about eagles gathering about a carcass — if only someone would help clean the window.

When we see the Story behind the text for the sermon, we make a discovery. The Story is not way back there — behind the ancient text. The Story is now. The Story behind the text is the Story that shines through the sermon *here*. The sermon is preached in Christian worship on a certain Sunday of the church year that has all the great events written all over it: Advent, Christmas, Epiphany, Lent, Easter, Pentecost. Seeing the Story now makes it fresh and immediate. The Story we see behind the text is the Story we celebrate behind the sermon, in and through worship here and now.

Text, sermon, listeners — all become part of the Story when it is seen and celebrated. Because we see the Story through sermon and text as being present here and now, we worship. We bring our praise, we confess our sins, we receive forgiveness, we pray for our neighbors and world, we give gifts, we bring new members to baptism, we eat and drink as signs of the new community and the coming kingdom. We see the Story not as spectators at a distance but as players in the cast. The more clearly we can see the Story, the more we know it is ours; the more we know it is ours, the more clearly we see it.

Sermons, like Bible texts, can conceal as well as reveal. Sermons are also smudged windows. But when we listen to sermons to see the Story, we can do a little window-cleaning ourselves. We can hold on to this part, clinging for dear life, let that part go, rearrange these words so we can hear and see better, correct that, celebrate this. Listening can keep us busy if we want to see the Story.

When we see and celebrate the Story of what God has done for us in Jesus Christ, we cannot be the same. Something happens to us. Elizabeth Achtemeier has seen what happens:

> biblical story becomes our story through our recall of it. . . . As God worked in and through Israel and Jesus Christ, so he uses the story of them to work the same way in our lives. What Israel was — the people accompanied by God — the Christian Church becomes, through the story. What Jesus Christ did — reconcile the world to God — his story continues to do for us, and indeed for all generations of Christians who will ever come after.[4]

David Buttrick offers a similar insight: "Like an untold adopted child suddenly told, you discovered a different identity by being given a new beginning. So, at minimum, preaching alters identity by prefacing *all* our stories and setting them in a larger story that stretches back to the dawn of God's creation."[5]

We cannot see and celebrate God's Story and remain unchanged. All the identities of age, gender, race, and class that function as barriers and weapons in a broken world are changed. They become gifts for serving because God's Story has given us a new identity. We are members of his

4. Achtemeier, *Creative Preaching* (Nashville: Abingdon Press, 1980), p. 18.
5. Buttrick, *Homiletic: Moves and Structures* (Philadelphia: Fortress Press, 1987), p. 11.

family on the way between creation and new creation. We are the people whose original address was Eden, who grieved our God with our rebellion, and whom God in the freedom of his grace calls his children anyway. We are the people who were brought down to bondage in Egypt, who were set free by God's outstretched arm, who settled in the promised land, who were escorted against our will to Babylon as exiles, who were released by an idol-worshiping servant of our God. We are the people Christ was born for, died for, lives again for. We are called the people of God not because of our wisdom or virtue or power but because God freely decided to be with us and for us. *That* Story gives us our identity.

With the identity comes our purpose. We are in God's world as God's people for God's purpose. From Abraham to David, through Christ to Paul, God's purpose was to bring the blessing of his grace to all the nations and to all of life. We are here "on purpose" now that we have seen the Story. We are witnesses of the Story and channels of its gifts.

Since our Story is centered in the cross of Jesus Christ, we are sustained by hope. The worst thing that could happen in the world has already happened — the crucifixion — and in the midst of that darkness God reconciled the world to himself. His resurrection is the assurance that his promise will prevail to make all things new.

When we listen to sermons, we have the right to see God's Story behind the text. The Story of what God has done for us in the history of Israel and in the person of Christ gives us our identity, purpose, and hope. Some Bible texts are brilliantly clear and astonish us again and again with what God has done. Blessed are those who hear sermons that do not obstruct the view. Other texts are smudged by cultural differentness, strange language, and bewildering events. Sermons can help us see the Story more clearly and fully through them.

The Story behind, in, and through the text and sermon lives behind, in, and through the people who see and celebrate it. Those who hear and see become living texts and sermons in the world. We become, as St. Paul said, "our letter of recommendation, written on your hearts, to be known and read by all men; and you show that you are a letter from Christ delivered by us, written not with ink but with the Spirit of the living God, not on tablets of stone but on tablets of human hearts" (2 Cor. 3:2-3).

When we listen to sermons, we have the right to see God's Story — if we dare.

— 5 —

The Story around the Text

THE BIBLE is an ancient book. Nearly twenty centuries have passed since its last words were written and nearly thirty centuries since its first words were written. That can be a problem.

When we come to listen to a sermon, we are in a hurry. We want to hear God's Word for here and now. We do not have the time, ability, or interest to hear a lecture about the language, culture, or habits of the ancient people among whom it was written. We come with a mix of holy and unholy impatience to hear what God says for now. Harry Emerson Fosdick's famous quip speaks for us: no one really comes to church with a burning interest in what happened to the Jebusites.

But not so fast. In our eagerness to hear a message for now, we must not ignore another pew right. When we listen to sermons, *we have the right to hear the story around the text*. Sermons that ignore the world in which the text lived and do not respect the distance between that world and our world are not likely to help us hear God's message now.

Sidney Greidanus calls one of his books *The Modern*

Preacher and the Ancient Text. The title and the book respect the distance between the past and the present. John R. W. Stott called his book on preaching *Between Two Worlds.* Both writers are concerned to speak and hear God's Word now; both writers respect the distance between the text and the pew.

When we simply and hastily collapse the distance between the two worlds, one of two disasters happens. First, some texts will remain forever out of our reach without meaning or message for our time. If the story of Moses striking the rock in the wilderness (Exod. 17:1-7) is told as though it happened last month in Arizona, it will leave us empty and bewildered. The distance is important if we are to hear message and meaning.

Second, ignoring the distance between text and pew tends to fill the text with irrelevant and even unfaithful meanings from our own time. The story of Eli the priest (1 Sam. 2:12-34) becomes merely an example of bad parenting instead of a story about God's incredible faithfulness when no hope for the future could be found within Israel. Jesus' parable of the talents (Matt. 25:14-30) becomes an endorsement of free enterprise, and the community of goods in the Pentecost church (Acts 2:44-45) is used to endorse communism.

When we ignore the distance between text and pew, the texts become silent or are filled with meanings they do not have. When we listen to sermons, we have a right to hear sermons that respect the distance between the world of the text and the world of the pew. We have the right to see enough of the story around the text so that we can hear God's Word in it here and now.

That distance is not just a problem; it is full of promise and possibility. The distance is there because God's message came to particular people in their own time, place, situation, and culture. Because God spoke then and there, the text holds promise that God can speak through it here and now.

Sidney Greidanus writes positively about the distance between the world of the text and today: "the challenge is to let the word of God address people today just as explicitly and concretely as it did in biblical times."[1]

How, then, shall we hear the distant text? What can sermons do for us that will respect the distance between text and pew so that we can hear God's Word from that text now?

Let's say that we are watching a football game on television. Our favorite wide receiver runs downfield, fakes out the defense, leaps, dives, and makes the catch of the year. Seconds later, we are treated to a replay. The film rolls to show us how the play developed, where the other players were, who made the key blocks, and what made the play so outstanding.

If that reception turned out to be the game-winning play, afterward we are "treated" to too many replays. The sequence is shown in slow motion to help us savor every second and inch of the play. Then views of the play are shown from the vantage point of four different cameras. Each one reveals (and conceals) different aspects of the action. One may use a wide-angle lens, another a zoom lens to show something special.

The next day the sports page splashes a picture of the receiver stretching to catch the ball while it is still three inches from his fingertips — a snapshot. It doesn't really

---

1. Greidanus, *The Modern Preacher and the Ancient Text* (Grand Rapids: William B. Eerdmans, 1988), p. 159.

tell the story, but because you saw the play and the replays, your imagination can supply the rest.

Sermons (and sermon titles) sometimes sound like they are describing snapshots. Here are Adam and Eve, Cain and Abel, Abraham and Lot, David and Nathan, Paul and Silas. It is true that Bible texts "freeze" the words and deeds of God and people in memorable pictures, but when we listen to a sermon, we want the moving picture replayed. We want slow motion where that will help. We need fresh angles on the action so that we can see what until now had escaped us. We want to see just enough of what came before, what followed, and what went on around the text. We have a right to see the story around the text so that we can get a good angle and the right distance to hear God's Word in and through it.

No sermon should attempt to answer all the possible questions about a text. Sermons are not lectures on biblical history, literature, theology, sociology, or geography. But when a sermon leads us into the text from one of these angles, the text can come alive and begin to move. Listeners who cultivate curiosity about the life situation of Bible texts will be prepared to enter the text from whatever direction the sermon provides.

Where is this text in Bible history? The stories of Cain and Abel, Noah, and the tower of Babel belong to the stage-setting stories of Genesis 1–11. But if these are stage-setting stories, and a sermon is preached from them, we have a right to hear something about what they are setting the stage *for.* The stories of Abraham, the exodus, the exile, the birth of Jesus, and Paul preaching in Athens all spring from different times in the unfolding of God's Story. That history can provide access to the text to help us see the story and hear the gospel.

The story of Ruth happened "In the days when the judges ruled" (1:1). So what? Is there a clue to the message of the story in that? The closing verses provide a brief genealogy, ending with "Obed of Jesse, and Jesse of David" (4:22). Bingo! Is that what the story is about? Is that the angle God wants us to see? In a time of multiple tragedies and disasters, when the future of God's family seemed to stall, God was building a bridge to a new future. And he used a foreigner to do it!

What other events is this text related to? Some events in Bible history tower above others and provide a way of seeing them. The call of Abraham, the move to Egypt under Joseph, the exodus, the conquest of Canaan, David's reign, and the exile and return are events that give meaning to the stories that precede and follow them. Israel's wilderness murmurings get meaning from the exodus, and the prophecy of Jonah attracts meaning from as far back as the call of Abraham, whose destiny was to bring blessing to all the families of the earth — including Nineveh. Why is that message so easily forgotten?

Sometimes the Bible itself directly relates earlier events to new situations. Paul remembered God's grace and Abraham's faith as he unfolded the gospel to the church at Rome (Rom. 4). He recalled the exodus as he wrote to the Corinthians about how to live in an idol-worshiping city as people whose lives were now nourished at the table of their Lord (1 Cor. 10:1-13). John told how Jesus spoke about the lifted-up serpent in the wilderness to describe his own mission (John 3:14-15). And who can miss the connection between Israel's murmuring about the diet in the wilderness and the leaders' murmuring at Jesus because he said, "I am the bread which came down from heaven" (John 6:41)?

We expect sermons to help us see where the text lives in God's story and how it is connected to other events and texts so that we can hear an intended Word from the Lord. Some of the links between events and texts are more subtle, but they are intended nonetheless. Who can read the story of Herod's slaughter of the innocents (Matt. 2:13-23) without seeing that Jesus is reliving Israel's history under Pharaoh? And who can hear the story of Abraham's readiness to sacrifice Isaac without seeing another Lamb of God being sacrificed in the place of others on a cross?

As we explore the story around the text to find angles of entry into it, another story is there. It is the story of the author, the first readers, and the reason for the writing. Who wrote it? To whom? And why? These are fair questions to ask of a text, and sermons should help us ask and answer them so that we can hear a true and faithful Word. These questions can be more easily and fully answered in some instances than in others, but all the answers we find provide ways to hear God's Word in the text.

We do not know who wrote Hebrews, but we know it was written to Jewish Christians who were having a hard time holding fast to their new faith. Galatians was written by Paul to a church or churches whose precise locations we do not know, but whose problem is clear: they had muffled the gospel of God's grace with the demands of the law. Romans was written by Paul to a church he had not yet visited but hoped to visit soon. He systematically proclaimed the gospel for Jew and Gentile and taught a faithful use of both law and liberty.

The Gospels provide a two-level story around their texts: the story of Jesus and the story of the churches to which the evangelists told the story of Jesus. The Gospel texts live when a sermon ushers us into those churches to

see Jesus as the misunderstood Messiah (Mark), the new
Moses (Matthew), the friend of the poor and powerless
(Luke), and the revealer of God (John).

When we listen to sermons, we have the right to see
the story or stories in which the texts live. The links of the
text to Bible history, to each other in that history, and to
authors and first readers provide angles from which to hear
the message of the text.

But Bible texts do not live only in history; they also
live in the world of literature. They are crafted writings.
Viewing the text as literature can provide entrances into
message and meaning in at least two ways: by helping us
see what kind of writing it is and where the text lives in
that writing.

The Bible is filled with different kinds of literature.
Reading the Proverbs is different from reading Romans.
The Psalms are different from the Gospels. Prophecy is not
the same kind of writing as the parables of Jesus. Sermons
that recognize, respect, reveal, and then *reflect* the kind of
text from which the message comes will remove barriers
to hearing the Word of God. A sermon from the Proverbs
should sound more like a grandmother talking to her
grandchildren about how life is put together than like a
politician trying to collect votes. A sermon from Psalm 8
should inspire awe. Jonah should catch us coming and
going in our own reluctance to see God's generosity ex-
tended to those who do not deserve it.

A sermon text has a context in the book of the Bible
from which it is drawn that can provide angles for us to
see the meaning. The doxology in Romans 11:33-36 con-
cludes Paul's teaching of Christian doctrine and introduces
his teaching about Christian behavior. Is that what doxologies are for? When Mark tells about the cleansing of

the temple, he sandwiches the story between Jesus' cursing the fig tree one day and the disciples' noticing that it was dead the next morning. Does the story of the fig tree interpret the cleansing of the temple? When the immediate context of a sermon text sheds light on it, sermon listeners have the right to follow that beam of light into the text to hear the message.

The history and literature in which a sermon text lives are important because they provide many possible angles for listeners to enter the text. But the story in which a text lives is also important for attempts to establish the right *distance* between the text and the pew. By "right distance" I mean that every Bible text is somehow related to our world, but no text was produced in our world. In fact, we may be inclined to suspect that some texts have nothing to do with our world. It is the task of the preacher to bring such texts close enough for the listeners to see and hear. We may be inclined to view some Bible texts as having sprung right out of our world last week. It is the preacher's task to push such texts far enough back that the listeners can establish a surer perspective and hear and see God's message in it. If a text is too far removed or too close, we will not be able to get the message. A sermon should establish the right distance between text and pew.

Some texts seem to fit so comfortably into our world that we miss their message. You have had a busy week. Besides all the usual demands of family and work, your in-laws spent half the week with you. It is now Sunday morning and you decide that you need some time alone to refresh yourself in quiet Bible reading and prayer. You have been meaning to read the Gospel of Mark again, and you decide this is the time to begin. You read chapter 1 about John the Baptist, the baptism of Jesus, the temptations in the wilderness, the opening of Jesus' ministry, the calling of some disciples, and the busy ministry in Capernaum. Jesus was busy, too! Then comes verse 35: "And in the morning, a great while before day, he rose and went out to a lonely place, and there he prayed."

How wonderful! The text fits perfectly into your world and life! Jesus and you were both busy, and you both felt the need for time to pray. God gave you just the right text for the day.

But wait a minute. Not so fast. What if "the lonely place" were called "wilderness" as it is in verses 3, 4, 12, and 13? If the lonely place were the wilderness where John the Baptist called for repentance and thus brought about a crisis, and where Jesus lived in conflict with Satan for forty days in the presence of wild beasts, then it did not much resemble the quiet place you sought out for reflection.

I can appreciate your need for quiet time, but this text is not about that. It is about temptation and struggle. It is about Jesus being tempted (and Simon Peter is the devil's agent again) to accept a call to Capernaum and settle down there and make good. Jesus could have become a successful religious leader with a good salary and benefits in Capernaum. The wilderness provided no rest. It was the place of struggle, conflict, and decision before the face of God.[2]

Other texts have become so familiar that we have tamed them. We read the parable of the Pharisee and the Publican in the temple (Luke 18:9-14) so often that we yawn and say, "Thank God I am not like the Pharisee," and do not even notice. Familiarity has removed the shock

---

2. See Thomas G. Long, "A Lonely Place," in *Shepherds and Bathrobes* (Lima, Ohio: CSS of Ohio, 1987).

from the story of the Good Samaritan, but imagine the leader of a feared street gang being held up as a model for how to be a neighbor! The story of the temple cleansing has been used too often against church sales and fund-raisers (I don't like them either) to speak its first message about making room for the nations in the place of prayer. And if we have been nurtured in certain traditions, when we read Luke 13:3 — "unless you repent you will all likewise perish" — we hear Jesus saying, "you will go to hell." Unless someone sets that text at least at arm's length, we will never hear that the word for "perish" is the same word for "lost" two chapters later in the stories of the lost sheep, coin, and son. In the light of these parables, "you will all likewise perish" means "you will get lost and I will have to find you too."

Other texts are too far removed from us to see and hear the message, some because of strange elements in the story that do not fit into our world or faith. We may need some help in bringing the "cows of Bashan" (Amos 4:1) within range of seeing, for example. We may need some help in getting a handle on the story of the unscrupulous steward in Luke 16:1-9. We may need some help in dealing with a juxtaposition of the neat, well-ordered world of Proverbs and the bleaker world of Ecclesiastes.

Other texts seem distant from us not because of what they contain but because we have moved too far away. You have just been inspired by a rousing sermon at an evangelistic meeting on Peter's great confession of faith: "you are the Christ, the Son of the living God" (Matt. 16:16). You are so inspired that you want to read more when you get home and go out and tell the world who Jesus is. So you read on: "then he strictly charged the disciples to tell no one that he was the Christ" (v. 20).

What is going on here? Will someone please bring me within hearing range?

Or you have just received training in how to witness. You have gone over all the rules about how to win friends and influence people. Then you read about the Canaanite woman who came begging for mercy for her daughter. Jesus brushed her off with a remark about not having been sent to her, followed by a putdown: "it is not fair to take the children's bread and throw it to the dogs" (Matt. 15:26). Is this the Jesus you want people to know? Will someone please help us hear the good news in that?

The Bible is an ancient book. We must accept and respect the distance between text and pew. Listeners need to hear the text from a helpful angle and from proper distance, not too close and not too far away. When we listen to sermons, *we have the right to see the story around the text.*

What the Text Says and Does

ORDINARILY, SERMONS are preached from Bible texts.

Preaching is *from* Bible texts. Not *on* Bible texts — although some sermons stay right there and never seem to leave the text. Not *about* Bible texts — although some sermons seem that distant and detached. Not *around* Bible texts — although some sermons seem to move in circles. Not *above* Bible texts — although some sermons travel in thin air. Not *under* Bible texts — although some sermons seem to be hiding. The word is *from*.

If a sermon is a bridge "between two worlds," as John R. W. Stott says, it will be spoken *from* Bible texts where they live *to* us where we live. A sermon spoken and heard will allow us to enter the text and the text to enter us. Listening to a sermon can bring what the text said and did into our life and world.

When we listen to sermons, we have the right to see the story behind the text, the story around the text, and *we have the right to hear the message of the text speak*.

Does every sermon need a Bible text? No, but ordinarily they do. St. Paul did quite well without a Bible text when he preached in Lystra (Acts 14) and in Athens (Acts

17). We can, perhaps, envision situations today in which a biblical sermon can be spoken without direct reference to a Bible text, but they will probably not be on a Sunday morning when Christians and other seeking sinners gather for worship. Ordinarily, in that situation, the sermon will need a Bible text.

When the sermon is about to begin, the preacher may say to the congregation, "Our text today is . . ." It is *our* text, though not everyone thinks so. The late James Daane, who was right about almost everything he said and wrote, disagreed. "Since the preacher must carve out the text, it should be referred to in the pulpit as 'my' text — not 'our' text. The minister, not the congregation, selected it."[1] But the scriptures and all the possible text selections in it belong to the church, not the preacher. This is especially apparent when, say, the common lectionary is used. The church which has received the scriptures schedules the cycle of readings, gives them to the preachers, and sends them to listen and speak on their behalf. "Our text today is . . ."

When the preaching text is identified and read, that act *interprets* what is about to happen. The sermon will be an attempt to say here and now what the text said then and there. Reading the text serves notice that the preacher is not being creative in the sense that he or she is making up a new message. The sermon will attempt to say what the text says, mean what the text means, and do what the text does.

When we prepare people to preach, we ask them to study "homiletics." Homiletics is the art of "saying the

---

1. Daane, *Preaching with Confidence: A Theological Essay on the Power of the Pulpit* (Grand Rapids: William B. Eerdmans, 1980), p. 60n.1.

same thing." When the text is read and announced as "our text," we can expect to hear the message of the text in and through the sermon.

Identifying the text also serves to *anchor* the sermon. Sermons that wander aimlessly through the Bible or through the condition of our world today are not anchored securely enough in the text. The text serves to tether the sermon to a center of meaning. This reminds me of the story of a preacher who was rambling from one thing to another and felt the congregation's attention slipping away. He tried to call them to attention by asking, "Do you get my drift?" He was greeted with a chorus of amens. We expect the sermon not to drift far from a field of meaning that is appropriate to the text.

The text also *gives direction* to the sermon. Bible texts were originally meant not only to say something but to *do* something. They were written to instruct, proclaim, comfort, disturb, promise, command, interpret, urge, call, reveal, forgive, save. While a text may well serve a different purpose in our world and life than it originally served, an effort on the part of the preacher to help us see the changed situation and the new function of the text can itself give direction to the sermon. That one text may serve different purposes in different situations is evident in the way Matthew and Luke report the story of the one lost sheep. In Matthew 18:10-14 the story calls for the practice of God's loving care in the church, while in Luke 15:3-7 the story explains why Jesus engaged in table fellowship with sinners.

Identifying and reading the Bible text before the sermon also *authorizes* what will be said in the sermon. The authority of the sermon itself depends on its faithfulness to the text, to those who hear, and to the Christ who comes to us in the hearing of the text and sermon. To prevent a misunderstanding of the authority of preaching in terms of worldly power and wisdom, those who listen to sermons and those who preach them will stay close to 1 Corinthians 1:18-25. There Paul calls Christ crucified the power and wisdom of God — weak and foolish though he seems. Preaching has authority (power and wisdom) insofar as it represents and proclaims the weakness and foolishness of Christ crucified.[2]

When we listen to a sermon, we have a right to hear the message of a Bible text *exposed*. Establishing a good angle and the right distance (Chap. 5) come to nothing if the sermon does not set the message of the text on display. Whether the message seems self-evident or mysterious when the text is read, the sermon should lift it up and bring it close so that we can see.

Perhaps we should consider allowing a few minutes of silence in worship after the sermon has been heard. In that silence worshipers could reflect immediately on a variety of questions: What was this sermon about? What was the message? Is the link between sermon and text clear? What will life be like if we believe this? What can we do about it? What did this sermon do to me? Some sermons call for the singing of a rousing hymn immediately; others may call for silence in which the text and sermon can do their saving work.

Whether in silence following the sermon or on the way home, in family table talk, or in reflective moments the next day, sermon listeners can ask their questions about a sermon and thereby make the message their own. The link between text and sermon is crucial. Assuming that the

2. See David Buttrick, *Homiletic* (Philadelphia: Fortress Press, 1987), pp. 245-46.

text is truly a literary unit (which every text should be), it has an intended message that should be exposed and displayed in the sermon. Sermon listeners have a right not only to see that message but to recognize the way it is linked to the text. If, following a sermon, the hearers cannot for the life of them recognize how *that* message came from *that* text, something has gone wrong somewhere.

Years ago I worshiped in a church in another state while I was on vacation. The parable of the Good Samaritan was read and identified as the text for the sermon. The preacher zeroed in on two words in Luke 10:31: "by chance." "Now by chance a priest was going down that road; and when he saw him he passed by on the other side." The preacher fixed our attention on those words by asking if anything *really* happens by chance. The sermon was about how much of life looks like happenstance, but in the end, God is at work to direct our paths. Nothing in the sermon showed the message of the text. The words could have come from any page in the Bible or from anywhere else. The message would have been the same. The sermon did not tell any lies, but it did not speak the truth of the text. The catchwords "by chance" were used to detach the sermon from the text.

Sermon listeners have a right to see an intended message of a text exposed to their view and to recognize the link between the text and sermon.

Sermon listeners also have the right to see an intended message of a text exposed to their view *where they are*. The message comes from an ancient text to listeners *here*. A sermon must span this gap. We can use such words as *trans*late, *trans*pose, *trans*fer, and *trans*port when describing what a sermon says and does.

Or we can say that a sermon should say *again* in our world what a text said and meant in its world. We can say that a sermon *re*interprets a text for now, *re*creates in our world what it was in its world, *re*states here and now the message proclaimed then and there.

If sermon listeners have a right to see the link between the text and the sermon, they also have a right to see the link between the sermon and their world.

Claiming this right on Sunday morning should be preceded by prayer for those who preach and listen to sermons. Here is the heart of the preaching-hearing task. Preparing to preach requires the preacher to negotiate the long distance between the world of the text and the world of the listeners. How does one travel from the world of St. Paul, whose preaching of the resurrection in Athens (Acts 17) brought a mix of mockery and hope, to our world, in which Easter is celebrated even by people who do not believe the resurrection? How does one negotiate the distance between Herodians and Zealots then and Republicans and Democrats now? How does one move from the Hebrew view of a person as a member of the community to the American view of society as a collection of individuals who are loosely joined together out of self-interest? How does one get from the world of the Psalms where rain flows from the hand of God to our weather forecasts that talk about jet streams and warm fronts? The road is long and dangerous.

But it is possible to make this journey. The God of the Bible is the God of all history. Human nature is what it was: bearing the image of God in our bent and broken world. The covenant community is continuous since the call of Abraham. The scriptures still do what they have always done: expose our human condition, reveal the saving grace of God, and call us into his family and service. And the Holy Spirit who inspired the scriptures is present in the church and world. The road is long, but the journey is possible.

How? How can a message get from the text to the pew? What can we listen for so that the message can come home?

We can listen for where the sermon is *aimed*. Sermons are messages aimed at something. Sometime at the beginning, in the middle, or toward the end of the sermon, we will see it. The sermon is aimed at comforting the grieving, disturbing the complacent, reassuring the perplexed, forgiving the sinner, offering hope to those in despair, calling the preoccupied to awareness or the sleepy to action, finding meaning in a tragedy. If we can see where the sermon is aimed, we may find ourselves right there in its path.

We can listen for *dialogue* in the sermon. I do not mean dialogue as a sermon form in which two or more persons hold a conversation while the congregation listens. I mean listening to your own questions about and responses to the sermon while you are listening to it. Chances are that the sermon will stir up questions arising out of your own faith and doubts and that it will somehow speak to them. You may find that the sermon will deliberately avoid addressing some questions. If you are understandably skeptical about the story of Jesus walking on the water and wonder how that can be, the sermon will do you no favor by addressing your skepticism head-on with talk about miracles then and now. Your questions will probably get bigger, and the message of the story will sail right past you. But *some* of your questions will be in dialogue with the sermon, and if the sermon ends while you have leftover questions, save them and bring them along next time.

We can listen for ways to *identify with* situations, events, and persons in the text and sermon. If a sermon is from Acts 10 in which God broke down the barrier between Jew and Gentile through Peter speaking the gospel of Jesus in the house of Cornelius, the situation, events, and persons in the story can keep us busy identifying with them. What do I hear if I put myself in the sandals of Cornelius or Peter or someone watching in the house? If the sermon is from the parable of the Pharisee and the Publican praying in the temple (Luke 18:9-13), it may invite us too soon and too easily to identify with the Publican. Try this instead: identify with those to whom the parable was addressed, "who trusted in themselves that they were righteous." Identifying with someone in a parable, and even taking turns with different characters, is a way of taking hold of the text and letting it explode its meaning right here and now. But when we do so, we should keep at hand a good warning: "the easiest mistake to make in identifying one's self with the text is to see it as a model for morality rather than a mirror for identity."[3]

When we listen to a sermon, we can watch for *pictures* that the text and sermon bring to us. The Bible is filled with images and stories that can be pictured on the mental screen of the listener. Some sermons transport biblical images directly into our world with enough familiarity that they do not need to be retouched. In spite of our distance from the world in which they were born, such images as "the Lord is my shepherd," "you are the body of Christ," and "we have an advocate with the Father" are familiar enough to recreate their meaning directly for most listeners.

3. William D. Thompson, *Preaching Biblically* (Nashville: Abingdon Press, 1980), p. 70.

However, some biblical images need to be recast if they are to communicate to us. An extreme example is the difficulty Bible translators have when they attempt to portray Christ as the Lamb of God in the language and culture of the Eskimos. There is simply nothing comparable in their experience or worldview.[4] Similarly, we need to have some biblical images retouched or remade if they are to communicate faithfully. If the image of God as judge evokes the picture of a black-robed, stern-faced person seated behind a courtroom bench with gavel raised, ready to pronounce the verdict in a criminal lawsuit, that image may work to prepare us for Romans 8:1: "There is therefore now no condemnation to those who are in Christ Jesus." But that image requires retouching if we are to understand the hopeful longing of a misunderstood and oppressed people whose day in court is finally coming: "Let the sea roar, and all that fills it; the world and those who dwell in it! Let the floods clap their hands; let the hills sing for joy together before the LORD, for he comes to judge the earth. He will judge the world with righteousness, and the peoples with equity!" (Ps. 98:7-9).

A fine example of recasting a biblical image so that its meaning and message can come home to us is found in Neal Plantinga's reflections on "the wrath of the Lamb":

> Years ago, as some friends and I were chatting one afternoon, our visit was interrupted by the screech of rubber on pavement and then the shouts of children. We hustled outdoors and found a golden cocker spaniel in the street, terribly run over, its back crushed, and screaming in a way you could never forget. This cocker, I later found out, was

4. See Ernest Best, *From Text to Sermon* (Atlanta: John Knox, 1978), pp. 33-35.

the gentle housepet of children across the street. As the dog writhed, a small girl tried to comfort it by placing her hand on the cocker's head. With what dying energy it had left, the cocker twisted around and, maybe for the first time in its life, tried to bite through that little girl's hand.

It was a chilling thing to see. You got the impression that a creature in death throes, a creature *in extremis,* a creature hurt beyond all endurance and decency had changed into a wholly different thing. It had become an alarming, mutant, wild-eyed creature who regarded comfort as an impertinence and wanted to suffer its death alone. . . .

In Revelation 5:5, John presents a striking juxtaposition of almost opposite animal images of Jesus Christ. In 5:5 "the lion of the Tribe of Judah" appears as royal conqueror. But (vs. 6) "then I saw a lamb, looking as if it had been slaughtered" (literally, "as if its throat had been slit"). In chapter 6 the images are blended into a jarring, fearful picture. Jesus Christ becomes a roaring lamb from whom people shrink. Who can stand before the wrath of a *lamb?*

In this horrifying image, John shows what we have done to God the Son. Some wire has gotten crossed in him. Some terrifying personality change has come over the lamb. Powerful human evildoers have turned God the Son from a mute victim into and almost mutant victor.[5]

When we listen to sermons, we can watch for images that dance in and around words and stories, sometimes straight from the text and sometimes retouched or recast for our use. We can watch for those images that the sermon awakens in us as we listen. We carry images in our memory

---

5. Plantinga, "The Wrath of the Lamb: A Good Friday Meditation," *Reformed Journal,* March 1988, p. 6.

that the sermon images can arouse. If the preacher re-
touches the image of the Good Shepherd by drawing com-
parisons to that one special teacher everyone seems to have
had, the one who made all the difference in your life, then
let that image recall Mr. Baber or Ms. Washington who
made your fifth grade a banner year. Images from text or
sermon can stir up images from our own lives that bring
the message and life together.

A sermon is not finished until it is heard. Listeners
finish the sermon by letting it into their lives — or sometimes by pulling hard on it to get it there. We can extend
this kind of welcome to the sermon by putting all that
matters to us on the table as we place ourselves in front
of the text. Our longings, fears, needs, sins, loves, joys,
doubts, faith, questions, and convictions all belong there
as we listen. Listening can keep us very busy. As the sermon
spans the distance between text and pew, listeners can be
kept busy imagining this, letting that go, rearranging these
pictures, holding on to that hope, promising to change,
and wondering afresh about mysteries old and new.

If we do this, then even after the sermon is done, the
message will not be finished with us. It will have entered
our life, and we will have been changed by it and by our
response to it. The message will live in us because it is the
message of the living Christ. The Word-made-flesh will
have entered our lives with the claims and promises of the
good news. We will have received our true identity and
mission from Christ through the text: he has made us his
witnesses who will be called upon to tell the truth about
what we have seen.

When we listen to sermons, *we have the right to hear
the message of the text here and now.*

— PART III —

. . . To Us in God's Story . . .

— 7 —

What's Happening?

IF YOU ARE OLD ENOUGH to remember the election of John F. Kennedy as president of the United States on November 1, 1960, you will even more vividly remember his assassination on November 22, 1963.

Where were you when you heard the news? Who told you? What was happening to people around you as they heard what happened? What did you do? How did you feel? Whom did you tell? Had they already heard?

When we rushed to watch the news on television, the film of the event itself was run and rerun until its images were burned indelibly in our memories and we grew numb. No wonder we can still see the motorcade, the sudden slouch of JFK, the reaction of the security guards, and the agony of the first lady. Television did that.

But many of us can still remember where and how we *heard* the news. Television did not record it. We were treated to no reruns — except in the privacy of our memories. And we can still see the place and people, and hear the words. I heard the words from a tearful cashier in a Florida restaurant who could not make change because she was sobbing, "They shot the president in Dallas."

That event was life-shaping. It changed the world in which we lived suddenly and traumatically. It changed us individually and communally because it brought about a crisis in which we had to make a response. The event and our responses to it changed us.

If you worshiped in a church on the following Sunday, chances are about 99 to 1 that you heard something there about what happened. Chances are that the preacher brought what happened into the light of God's Story from a Bible text. God's Story gave us time and space to grieve, rage, fear, grope for meaning, find comfort, hope, and trust.

If that is what you experienced on that Sunday, another of your pew rights was respected: when we listen to sermons, *we have the right to see what's happening in the light of God's Story.*

This right is rooted in the heart of the good news from God — namely, that Jesus is the Christ. To believe that Jesus is the Christ is to believe that history has a center in him and that his light reaches backward, forward, and all around. To believe that Jesus is the Christ is to love to hear and tell "the old, old story," as the hymn has it. But the old story gives light that can help us see and respond to what's happening now. When we listen to sermons that proclaim Jesus as the Christ, we can expect to see what's happening in the light of what happened then. Though we may yet see as through a glass darkly, we will catch glimpses of how to wait, watch, worship, and work in the midst of this week's news.

The central issue that runs through the four New Testament Gospels is this: Who is this Jesus of Nazareth? As that question was asked and answered time and time again by all sorts of people, it came down to this: Is Jesus the Christ? That is the decisive question in the Gospels.

The stakes were high. If Jesus is the Christ, then history has a new center. The blessing promised to and through Abraham is now let loose among the nations. If Jesus is the Christ, the Old Covenant is fulfilled and the New Covenant creates the new people of God.

James Daane saw it and said it:

> the truth that Jesus is the Christ . . . [is] the central affirmation of the New Testament, the core of the early church's proclamation, the theme of Peter's Pentecost sermon. For preaching Jesus as the Christ, the early apostles were arrested and jailed, and on being beaten and released, did it again. "Every day in the temple and at home they did not cease teaching and preaching *Jesus as the Christ*" (Acts 5:42). For preaching that God had elected him whom his hearers had rejected, Stephen became the first Christian martyr. It was the belief that Jesus is the Christ, the chosen of God, that led Saul to lay waste the church of Jerusalem and to journey to Damascus to attack the Christians there; and it was the demonstration that Jesus is the Christ on his way to Damascus that triggered his conversion.[1]

The faith that Jesus of Nazareth is the Christ of God is a conviction that gives history its center and meaning. *Our* history. When we listen to sermons, we have the right to see *our* history in the light of history's center, Jesus the Christ.

Sermons that are cut loose from the time, place, and situation of the listeners create barriers to seeing God's Story in Christ and in what's happening now. Helmut Thielicke preached from the Lord's Prayer under precarious

1. Daane, *The Freedom of God* (Grand Rapids: William B. Eerdmans, 1973), p. 118.

conditions in Stuttgart during the "horrors of the air raids, the declining days of a reign of terror, and finally through the period of total military and political collapse" of the Third Reich.[2] His published sermons bear the marks of the situation in which they were heard.

But Thielicke reports with some distress that following the war, some preaching was totally unaffected by what the church had been through.

> It was an experience that was confirmed again and again at numerous conferences with prominent men of the church. We met many pastors who had returned from long military service or long and grievous imprisonment. Both of these experiences had confronted them with the boundary situations of human life and subjected them to an exceedingly elemental fate. They had been forcibly ejected from the ecclesiastical ghetto and exposed to the directest kind of human contacts. Everybody thought that this would have a very discernible effect upon the way they preached. If before they had perhaps been rather colorless and withdrawn from life, now surely they would be vital and saturated with the juices of suffering and real life. That hope increased as one listened to them recounting their experiences; everything they said was taut and compact, there was no false tone, and therefore we were stirred. But once they were in the pulpit, all this immediacy disappeared. The same old dull monotonous waters flowed down the same old accustomed channel. Even that which still retained the tone of immediacy, the man's own personal tone, had again become general and colorless. And whereas we used to be inclined to think that "the whole man had been recast and transformed in the fires of war," in the

2. Thielicke, *Our Heavenly Father* (1960; reprint, Grand Rapids: Baker Book House, 1974), p. 13.

pulpit he appeared to go on without any perceptible break from where he had left off in 1939.[3]

If that happens to *preachers* when sermons ignore life experience, what happens to listeners? How can one know, love, tell, and celebrate God's Story if sermons ignore what happened in the war and, instead, pour "the same old dull monotonous waters . . . down the same old accustomed channel"?

But what kind of experiences can be brought to the light of Jesus Christ that we may see God's Story in ours more clearly? There are at least three sources of experience to watch: life-shaping events, life's changing seasons, and life-enriching stories.

A life-shaping event changes our circumstances and requires a response. The assassination of John F. Kennedy was such an event. A change occurred immediately in the loss of our elected president, and again when Lyndon B. Johnson was sworn in as president aboard Air Force One on the way to Washington. But we were also shaped by our responses to the event. The initial response was like the dread expressed by the jailer in Philippi who fell down before Paul and Silas pleading, "What must I do to be saved?" (Acts 16:30). Newscasters, with voices quivering, were at a loss for words, and although the debate about prayer in public schools was at fever pitch, some said, "All we can do is pray." Responses included fear, compassion, cynicism, hope, anger, and more. We were shaped by the event and by our responses to it.

When the world saw people from East and West

3. Thielicke, *The Trouble with the Church* (New York: Harper & Row, 1965), pp. 6-7.

Berlin dancing on the wall before it was broken down in October 1989, we were changed by the event and by our responses to it. In a world that had come to expect oppression and alienation, this sign of freedom and reconciliation was life-shaping. Similarly, in August 1991 a wire service showed a picture of a child playing on a statue of Lenin that was lying face down in a square in Kiev. It was a sign of a life-shaping event.

Life-shaping events may bring lamentations, celebrations, or both. The events may be local, congregational, national, or international. They may be invasions, truces, earthquakes, drought-ending rains, murders in the neighborhood, deaths, births, marriages, divorces. Life-shaping events — whether local or global — can be brought to the light of history's center, Jesus the Christ.

What can we hope to see in the light of Jesus the Christ? We can hope to see through the life-shaping events to the fact that at the center of history is a crucifixion and resurrection, and at the heart of life is God-with-us in all our lamentations and celebrations. In spite of how we might feel at the moment, we can see that our life-shaping events are not ultimate. The Christ wraps our lamentations in hope and calls us to new celebrations. The Christ restrains our celebrations with compassion for those yet oppressed and sends us off to find other walls that need to come down. Jesus the Christ shows us what is ultimate in the life-shaping events and refashions our responses to them with hope and compassion.

In 1971 a life-shaping event occurred in the United Presbyterian Church. A report to the General Assembly disclosed that $10,000 had been granted from its legal defense fund for poor and minority people to defend Angela Davis, a communist who was accused of murder. The

event made national news, and "rocked Presbyterian congregations across the country to their foundations."[4]
Nearly every Presbyterian who attended worship heard the
event addressed in a sermon during the ensuing two weeks
and had some initial reaction to it.

In 1978 a Princeton Seminary student examined a
sampling of sermons preached in response to that event.
Presumably, Presbyterian preachers were seeking to bring
the light of Jesus the Christ to that life-shaping event for
Presbyterians. The student learned, among other things,
that the preachers operated on a considerable variety of
assumptions about the kind of community the listeners
were. Quite apart from their own position on the issue of
the grant, the preachers assumed that the listeners fell into
one of five kinds of communities: (1) a community of
protesters who needed to be calmed or incited, (2) a community that was seeking information and understanding,
(3) a community concerned about the meaning of denominational affiliation, (4) a community that was seeking to
"do justice," or (5) a community of wounded people who
needed healing. Few of the preachers thought consciously
about the kind of community of people they were addressing, but the sermons tended to create the kind of community the preacher assumed them to be. If the preacher
assumed that they were a community of protesters who
needed to be incited to "do something about it," they
tended to become that. If the preacher assumed them to
be a community of wounded people who needed to be
healed, they tended to become that. Now it appears that
bringing a life-shaping event to the light of Jesus the Christ

4. J. Randall Nichols, *Building the Word* (San Francisco: Harper
& Row, 1980), p. 110.

is not as simple as it seemed at first. The preacher's assumptions about who and where the listeners are may focus the light in different ways and may reshape the listeners' response to the event.

Imagine yourself a Presbyterian in that situation. You come to worship hopping mad about the report that $10,000 has been given to defend Angela Davis, a communist accused of murder. The sermon, however, assumes that you are seeking information and proceeds to give it. Or you come seeking information, and the sermon assumes you are wondering what it means to be part of the Presbyterian church. Or you are wondering about whether being independent is better than being Presbyterian, and the sermon assumes that you are struggling desperately over the question of what it means to "do justice." Or you come wanting to "do justice," and the preacher assumes that you need healing.

In a time when life-shaping events such as denominational actions and decisions tend to fragment the church into many different minds, what can a listener do? I would suggest that these situations offer a special opportunity. Provided that the sermon itself is rooted in and authorized by a Bible text (which all the sermons suggested above could be), listening to sermons that are off center from where we are offer us the opportunity to listen with the ears and eyes of our brothers and sisters. If you are angry, but the sermon addresses you as though you are hurt, put yourself in the place of someone who hurts for just a little while. If you are wondering what "doing justice" means, but the sermon treats you as though you wonder what being Presbyterian obligates you to do, give some consideration to those obligations for just a little while. Such sermons can nudge us to examine our own responses to an event and invite us to reshape our responses in company with our brothers and sisters in Christ.

Not every sermon has to hit us directly to bless us; sometimes listening with the ears of a neighbor will bring us unexpected grace.

Life-shaping events are often sudden, radical, disruptive, and traumatic. At the other end of what's happening is the experience of living through life's changing seasons. Silently, surely, and subtly, we are all moving through the seasons of life from infancy, childhood, adolescence, youth, and middle age to old age. When we listen to sermons, we can bring this experience of life's seasons to the light of history's center: Jesus the Christ.

The experience comes at different times and in different ways. A child stands before a mirror and, for the first time, tries to see herself as others may see her. She is "aging." A thirteen-year-old boy tries to hide his embarrassment when his changing voice cracks. A college freshman weighs the choice between marriage and career or wonders how to balance them. A thirty-five-year-old saleswoman finds that the company isn't making any allowances for her "youth" anymore, and the pressure to produce and succeed are doubled. Is this her experience of "middle age"? A fifty-five-year-old mails in his application for membership in the American Association of Retired Persons and laughs about it but worries about what retirement and old age will really be like.

There are many ways to identify and organize the seasons of life, but the boundaries are not rigid or clear. Whether we are guided by Erik Ericson's "life cycle" or Gail Sheehy's "passages," we bring the experience of life's changing seasons when we listen to sermons. We will not hear a model for how-to-live-through-life's-stages-as-Jesus-did; there is no such model. But we do have the testimony of the apostles to his birth, ministry, death, and resurrection. That Story has the same disturbing and reassuring impact on our experience of life's seasons as it has on the experience of life-shaping events: the message is that none of the seasons (or events) is ultimate. What is ultimate is the Story of what God has said and done for us in the death and resurrection of Jesus the Christ. The grace of God-with-us from birth to death in Jesus Christ attends us in all the stages of life.

If we bring our experience of life's changing seasons when we listen to sermons, we will be empowered to live creatively through those seasons. We will reject the values of our society that sentimentalizes children (they are so innocent), idolizes and scourges youth (they are models of how to look, but not of how to behave), pressurizes middle age (you should have succeeded and solved all the problems you inherited by now), and patronizes the elderly (take advantage of our senior citizen discounts). Instead, we can follow the lead of Walter Burghardt's mature reflections on life in *Seasons that Laugh or Weep: Musings on the Human Journey*. He brings the light of Jesus the Christ to the seasons of life and calls them Spring, Summer, Autumn, and Winter. Spring is that childhood (and adolescent) season of vulnerability that calls for love. Summer is early adulthood, which brings crisis and decision, struggle and a search for identity. Autumn is late adulthood, when we are trapped in our own questionings and calls for genuine spirituality. Winter is old age, when the need for integration and wholeness can lead to contemplation ("a long, loving look at the real"). Such reflections enable us to see the seasons of life as channels for the grace of Jesus the Christ.

When we listen to sermons, we want to see what's

happening in the light of Jesus the Christ. And so we bring life-shaping events, life's changing seasons, and life-enriching stories in order to see them more clearly.

Life-enriching stories are simply tales that are important to the listeners. We all have a vast library of stories that we bring along to worship. Some are about what we have experienced personally in our brief or long life. Some are the stories of others that we have heard or seen or read. When we listen to sermons, recollections of these stories are stirred by hearing God's Story. We remember them and see them again in a new light, finding new meanings in them. The stories that the preacher brings to the sermon to show how God's Story illumines our story are important. But we have stories, too, and they have the capacity not only to illustrate the message of the text but also to receive new meaning themselves when we view them in the light of God's Story in Jesus the Christ.

When we hear about the series of tragic losses suffered by Naomi in the opening chapter of Ruth, we will recall stories of similar tragedy that are stored in our memory. When we hear the story of the prodigal son and his father and brother, we will recall stories of alienation and reconciliation that are stored in our memory — some of which are still unresolved. The preacher has work to do to bring God's Story to our stories, but we as listeners also have work to do to bring our stories to God's. When we view our stories in the light of Jesus the Christ, we experience in new ways the fact that our own life and times are part of God's continuing Story.

The preacher may need to bring stories from the church's past to help us see what's happening now. These stories may not be part of the listener's mental library, but they can be helpful as we try to see our present story in the light of the deep and long history of the church. When we face a doctrinal debate, it may help to hear that it took the church almost five centuries to hammer out an agreement about a point we take for granted — namely, that God is Father, Son, and Holy Spirit and that Jesus Christ is fully human and fully divine. When we face church-state issues, it may help to hear that our situation of freedom of religion in a pluralistic society is so new that it hardly registers on the twenty-century-long calendar of the church. When we are tempted to mount crusades to enforce moral orthodoxy with political power, it may help to hear about earlier crusades of which we have repented and to be reminded that the true power of the church lies in telling God's Story. Seeing our present in the light of the past can encourage and reassure us by reminding us that others have been in places similar to those in which we find ourselves now.

Those who preach sermons and those who listen to them bring stories that get new meaning from God's Story centered in Jesus the Christ. Just for practice, here is a story to add to your library and bring with you to the next time you listen to a sermon. Bring this story to the light of Jesus the Christ and watch what you see:

> One December afternoon many years ago a group of parents stood in the lobby of a nursery school waiting to claim their children after the last pre-Christmas class session. As the youngsters ran from their lockers, each one carried in his hands the "surprise," the brightly wrapped package on which he had been working diligently for weeks. One small boy, trying to run, put on his coat, and wave, all at the same time, slipped and fell. The "surprise" flew out of his grasp, landed on the tile floor, and broke with an obvious ceramic crash.

The child's first reaction was one of stunned silence. But in a moment he set up an inconsolable wail. His father, thinking to comfort him, knelt down and murmured, "Now it doesn't matter, son. It really doesn't matter."

But his mother, much wiser in such affairs, swept the boy into her arms and said, "Oh, but it does matter. It matters a great deal." And she wept with her son.[5]

You may have to listen to several sermons before you get the right light, but when you do, watch the meanings come to life.

If Jesus is the Christ as the Gospels proclaim, then he is the center of history who sheds light backward, forward, and all around. Listening to sermons that are spoken in his name, we can look for light on life-shaping events, life's changing seasons, and life-enriching stories. When we listen to sermons, *we have the right to see what's happening in the light of God's Story.*

5. The story was originally told by William Muehl and reported by J. Randall Nichols in *Building the Word: The Dynamics of Communication and Preaching* (San Francisco: Harper & Row, 1980), p. 11.

— 8 —

Two Pairs of Spectacles

JOHN CALVIN is known for comparing the Bible to a pair of eyeglasses: "just as eyes, when dimmed with age or weakness or by some other defect, unless aided by spectacles, discern nothing distinctly; so, such is our feebleness, unless Scripture guides us" (*Institutes,* 1.14.1). Without the Bible, says Calvin, we cannot see clearly.

The problem, however, is that we are already wearing a pair of spectacles. Our ways of living, speaking, choosing, working, playing, marrying, and parenting already incline us toward looking at the world and life in certain ways. Our culture — that is, our shared ways of living together — determines to a considerable degree how we look at the world, how we read the Bible, and what we see when we do.

Is it possible to trade in the spectacles supplied by our culture for those supplied by the Bible? Or is it possible to wear two pairs at once? The question is important because *when we listen to a sermon, we have the right to see our culture in the light of God's Story.*

We do have a real problem here. When we listen to a sermon, our culture is powerfully present. It is present in the language that is spoken, the illustrations that are proffered, the applications that are made, and the meanings that are inferred. A sermon cannot be spoken or heard from outside the culture in which we live. How then can we see our culture in the light of God's Story when the sermon we are hearing is embodied in our culture? Can a sermon that uses the spectacles supplied by our culture to see God's Story also use the spectacles supplied by the Bible to see our culture?

To change the picture, one writer who attempts to see cultures in the light of God's Story has been accused by critics of "trying to push a bus while we are sitting on it."[1] When we listen to a sermon, we have the right to see our culture in the light of God's Story. But is that possible?

It begins to appear possible when we look at how we receive God's Story. It comes to us in the Bible, which spans many centuries and can be traced through vast cultural changes. From the journeys of Abraham to Israel's oppression in Egypt to the exodus, the wilderness, and the promised land, God's Story has already happened in and through cultural changes — and it has only just begun. The days of the judges, kings, prophets, exile in Babylon, and restoration weave the Story through changing scenes that seem to have little in common. The New Testament begins in the days of Caesar Augustus, whose collection of taxes set the stage for the birth of Jesus in Bethlehem, and it ends with the apostle John in exile on the Isle of Patmos, singing new songs about the victory of the Lamb who was slain. The Story is told in and through many cultural changes but is never limited or reduced to any one. The way we

1. See Lesslie Newbigin, *The Gospel in a Pluralist Society* (Grand Rapids: William B. Eerdmans, 1989), pp. 95 and 191.

receive God's Story in the Bible gives a clue as to how it is possible for us to see our own culture in its light.

More importantly, God's Story has a center. In the death and resurrection of Jesus Christ, all the cultures of the world are exposed and the victorious grace of God is revealed. When Jesus was crucified, it was at the hands of those who represented the culture. The religious and political powers joined forces against Jesus and sent him to the cross. In the light of what happened at Calvary, the best of whatever any culture can promise stands exposed as rebellious and arrogant. The ground at the cross is level — not only for individuals but for the cultures of the world. Anyone from any culture who sees the cross of Jesus as the center of history will thereby be prevented from looking down on other cultures or elevating his own as the standard for others.

But God raised Jesus from the dead and unleashed the good news of the forgiveness of sins and the infinite goodness of God. The resurrection of Jesus is God's resounding Yes to the world — including the cultures of the world. If the cross of Jesus shows us that our culture cannot save us, the resurrection of Jesus reveals that our culture is not beyond the reach of God's victorious love.

It is possible for us to see our culture in the light of God's Story because that Story, at its center, is God's No and Yes to culture. In the words of Lesslie Newbigin,

> if this biblical interpretation of the human story, with its center in the double event of Jesus' death and resurrection, is our clue, then it will follow that we are called neither to a simple affirmation of human culture nor to a simple rejection of it. We are to cherish human culture as an area in which we live under God's grace and are given daily

new tokens of that grace. But we are called also to remember that we are part of that whole seamless texture of human culture which was shown on the day we call Good Friday to be in murderous rebellion against the grace of God. We have to say both "God accepts human culture" and also "God judges human culture."[2]

We are wondering how it might be possible to listen to a sermon from within a culture and still see that culture in the light of God's Story. We can find a way by looking at how we received the Story in and through the many cultures of the Bible and by focusing on the death and resurrection of Jesus as the center of the Story that judges and accepts human culture.

Furthermore, as the Story unfolds in the New Testament, a central theme is the power of the gospel of Jesus Christ to unite Jew and Gentile in the one church. For the sake of bringing the promised blessing to all the nations, God separated Israel from the nations. But in Christ the separation was overcome. Acts tells how the gospel was brought from Jerusalem to Rome, and it shows how the cultures it met along the way were judged and accepted in its light.

The stories of Peter in Acts 10 and of the council in Jerusalem in Acts 15 are important evidences of the power of the gospel to cross cultural barriers. Peter had trouble seeing how Gentiles could become Christians without first becoming Jews, so God gave him a vision and a mission. God presented Peter with a vision of clean and unclean food and commanded him to eat what had been forbidden. Then he was given the mission of visiting an "unclean" Gentile named Cornelius in the town of Caesarea. When

2. Newbigin, *The Gospel in a Pluralist Society,* p. 195.

Peter spoke the gospel of Jesus Christ in the house of a
Gentile, the Story cut two ways: Peter and Cornelius, Jew
and Gentile — both were changed. God's Story had power
to cross the boundary and shed the light needed to judge
and accept both cultures.

In Acts 15 the church was in crisis. The Gentiles were
receiving and believing the gospel, but that news disturbed
the church leaders in Jerusalem. They could not imagine
Gentiles becoming Christians without first becoming Jews.
The debate provided Peter with his finest moment. He
spoke the gospel as the Jerusalem church needed to hear
it, as though for the first time: "But we believe that we
[Jews] shall be saved through the grace of the Lord Jesus,
just as they [the Gentiles] will" (Acts 15:11). God's Story,
centered in the death and resurrection of Jesus Christ, is
the light in which all culture is judged and accepted.

The outcome of that Story sheds its light on all human
culture. Isaiah 60 gives us a vision of the goal and destiny
of the kingdom of God: "nations shall come to your light,
and kings to the brightness of your rising" (v. 3). As the
vision is enlarged, "the wealth of the nations shall come
to you" (v. 5). The picture is about the outcome of God's
Story in which all the nations and cultures will bring their
gifts into the kingdom of God. All idolatry, arrogance, and
corruption will be judged and left behind, and God's splen-
did kingdom will radiate with the astonishing riches of all
the nations.[3] The vision of Isaiah is magnified in the Revelation of St. John, who celebrates the coming of a kingdom
that includes people "from every tribe and tongue and
people and nation" (5:9).

3. For more on this, see Richard Mouw, *When the Kings Come
Marching In* (Grand Rapids: William B. Eerdmans, 1983).

Is it possible to see our culture in the light of God's Story while listening to that story from within our culture? Yes. The record of the Story in the culturally diverse Bible, the center of the Story in the death and resurrection of Jesus, the progress of the Story in overcoming the ancient Jew-Gentile barrier, and the outcome of the Story in the culture-rich, restored kingdom of God all affirm this possibility.

If, when listening to a sermon, we have the right to see our culture in the light of God's Story, just what will we be looking for? What will we need to see in order to live God's Story within our own culture?

In order to live faithfully, we need to see when and where to say Yes, No, and Maybe as participants in God's Story and in our culture. We will listen to sermons the way the first readers of the Gospels and Epistles listened to them — to see how to live their new life in Christ in Rome, Corinth, or Ephesus. Hearing gave them light to see, and seeing gave them power to say Yes, No, and Maybe in ways that gave shape to their lives and their culture and made God's Story visible in the world. Lesslie Newbigin's understanding of culture in the light of the death and resurrection of Jesus Christ led him to say that "God accepts human culture" and also that "God judges human culture." Listening to sermons should help us see the difference.

Our North American culture opposes belief in the incredible news of God's Story. Our culture places us under daily obligation to earn everything that the good life requires. We earn our pay, we earn our grades, we work to deserve our job, we try to achieve success, we strain to win games, customers, and wars. The popular television ad that says "We make money the old-fashioned way — we *earn* it" reflects a deeply held cultural conviction.

But when we hear God's Story announcing to us that we are forgiven and redeemed by the sheer mercy and grace of God made known in Jesus Christ, something has to give. Either the Story is overcome by the cultural belief or the belief is overcome by the Story. Listening to sermons can help us see the truth that we all live on welfare — the welfare of God's grace in Christ. When we see that, we will receive power to say Yes and No in faithful ways.

The culture does not merely provides obstacles to and opportunities for believing the truth of God's Story; it can also help and hinder the *telling* of the Story. There is no way to hear, believe, or tell the Story without culture — without language, for example. But the church has learned from painful and sometimes shameful experience that God's Story is not identical to the cultural forms in which it is embodied. God has used cross-cultural missions to bring the good news to many in spite of the disgraceful treatment of people and cultures that often accompanied the news. Cross-cultural mission — both domestic and overseas — provides too many examples of how missionaries confused God's Story with their own culture.

Eugene Nida, himself a sensitive veteran missionary to India for many years, tells about a young Liberian Christian who in due time was ordained to be a minister of the gospel among his people. How did he show the prestige appropriate to his new appointment? He spoke in English through an interpreter — even though he was speaking to his own people![4]

Listening to sermons can help us see ways in which our culture can help or hinder the telling of God's Story.

4. Nida, *Customs and Cultures* (New York: Harper & Row, 1954), p. 255.

The seeing can empower us to say Yes and No to the culture in ways that will free us for a more faithful telling.

Believing, telling, and living God's Story can happen only within human culture. The history of God's people from Abraham to the present assures us that there are no cultural conditions that can either guarantee or prevent the living of the Story. Persecution and oppression have not destroyed the Story or quenched the community of faith. Nor has national favor or cultural privilege. The church lives by remembering, retelling, and reenacting the Story through the seasons of the church year around the Bible and the table.

However, we must take care to watch out for the subtle ways in which the culture seeks to co-opt the church into serving purposes that are foreign to God's Story. Lesslie Newbigin, who spent forty years in India, saw the danger:

> a missionary in India learns to realize that there are certain ways of understanding the world that are so fundamental that they have never been questioned in all the revolutions of Indian thought from the Buddha to the Mahatma, from Gautama to Gandhi. I mean, for example, the doctrines of *karma* and *samsara* which see human life in terms of the wheel of nature, the endless cycles of birth, growth, decay, death, and then a new birth. That is, strictly speaking, the "natural" way to understand human life — the life of the individual and the life of nations. Within this view it is therefore inconceivable that the life of one man at a particular point in history could permanently alter the state of things. Jesus can illustrate the truth about the human condition, but he cannot change it. And so, . . . a portrait of Jesus can be happily accommodated in the premises of a Hindu missionary establishment, because Jesus has been

painlessly incorporated into the Hindu worldview. The foreign missionary knows that this is not the conversion of India but the co-option of Jesus, the domestication of the gospel into the Hindu worldview. He only slowly begins to realize that the same thing has happened in the West. Jesus is understood in the light of the assumptions which control our culture.[5]

The same thing has happened in the West. It is easier for us to see how Jesus can be used to illustrate a Hindu worldview that is foreign to God's Story than it is to see how it happens among us. But listening to sermons can help us see how God's Story can be co-opted and made to serve cultural values, utopian dreams, or national purposes that are foreign to the Story itself.

In 1960 the presidential campaign between John F. Kennedy and Richard M. Nixon was heating up. The issue that fired the debate was whether it was "safe" to have a Roman Catholic in the White House. The Catholic teaching that places national identities and loyalties second to the Church and the institutional relationship between Kennedy's Church and the Vatican triggered fearful and angry opposition to his candidacy. When Republican president Dwight D. Eisenhower finally entered the debate, he did not oppose Kennedy's candidacy on "religious" grounds. All of us, he said, including Kennedy, are first of all Americans.

Eisenhower was right in not opposing Kennedy's candidacy, but his reason was inadequate at best and dangerous at worst. He implied that religious beliefs are a private matter and either have nothing to do with public life or are subservient to a national ideology. He gave first place

5. Newbigin, *The Gospel in a Pluralist Society,* p. 96.

to "America" and saw religious convictions as privately held supports for the state. Whether a picture of Jesus is used to endorse a Hindu worldview in the East or religion is used to support national ideology in the West, God's Story has been co-opted and can no longer function as a critic of the worldview or ideology.

When Eisenhower said that we are Americans first, he was giving voice to a widely held nationalist creed. It is not surprising, then, that such an ideology should catch its share of criticism from people who have lived deeply in God's Story. Note the similarity in the titles of two radical critiques of the American ideology: in 1969 William String-fellow published *An Ethic for Christians and Other Aliens in a Strange Land,* and in 1989 Stanley Hauerwas and William Willimon published *Resident Aliens: Life in the Christian Colony.*

Hauerwas and Willimon note that the cozy coalition between church and state that began under Constantine in A.D. 313 was not just a matter of the church endorsing state actions; it was also a matter of the state undertaking the church's role in inappropriate ways. Willimon writes that for him this tangled relationship came to an end in a symbolic way

> sometime on a Sunday evening in 1963. Then, in Green-ville, South Carolina, in defiance of the state's time-honored blue laws, the Fox theater opened on Sunday. Seven of us — regular attenders of the Methodist Youth Fellowship at Buncombe Street Church — made a pact to enter the front door of the church, be seen, then quietly slip out the back door and join John Wayne at the Fox.
>
> That evening has come to represent a watershed in the history of Christendom, South Carolina style. On that night, Greenville, South Carolina — the last pocket of re-

sistance to secularity in the Western world — served notice
that it would no longer be a prop for the church. There
would be no more free passes for the church, no more free
rides. The Fox Theater went head to head with the church
over who would provide the world view for the young.
That night in 1963, the Fox Theater won the opening
skirmish.[6]

There are those who mourn the death of Christendom, the end of the alliance between church and state in
which each served the ends of the other. Hauerwas and
Willimon, on the other hand, celebrate the death of the old
arrangements: "the loss of Christendom gives us a joyous
opportunity to reclaim the freedom to proclaim the gospel
in a way in which we cannot when the main social task of
the church is to serve as one among many helpful props
for the state."[7]

There is no way to believe, tell, or live God's Story
outside of culture, but this is not to say that we cannot
distinguish between the two. Listening to sermons can help
us see our culture so that we can believe, tell, and live the
Story more faithfully.

I suggested earlier that listening to sermons can help
us see when and where to say Yes, No, and Maybe to the
culture. The "maybe" is important because no one knows
the Story so completely or sees the culture so clearly that
our responses can be reduced to just Yes or No. Jesus
compared the coming of the kingdom of God to a farmer
whose crop yields its fruit quietly and surely, though "he
knows not how" (Mark 4:27). And when the apostle Paul

6. Hauerwas and Willimon, *Resident Aliens: Life in the Christian
Colony* (Nashville: Abingdon Press, 1989), pp. 15-16.
7. Hauerwas and Willimon, *Resident Aliens*, pp. 38-39.

labored mightily to show the Corinthian Church how to live God's Story in their city, he helped them see where to say Yes and No to common cultural situations, but he also included Maybe (1 Cor. 7:25). God's Story is too profound and our culture is too complex to reduce our responses to a simple Yes or No in all situations. A willingness to say "maybe" can be a sign of humility, patience, and trust until we see more clearly.

Listening to sermons can help us see the culture in which the Bible text originally lived. It can help us see how God's Story was lived in cultures of the past. But when we listen to sermons, we also have the right to see *our* culture in the light of God's Story.

But what, then, can we expect to see? What features of our culture can we expect to be exposed to the light of the Story?

Many descriptions and lists are available to us, and none can be complete. Nearly every list, however, will identify individualism as a powerful feature of our North American culture. The book that caught wide attention in 1985 was *Habits of the Heart,* a study of individualism and commitment in American life by sociologist Robert Bellah and his colleagues. In its purist form, individualism exalts the individual person to the place of greatest reality and highest value. Society, community, takes a back seat to the concerns of the individual. In fact, radical individualists maintain that society is nothing more than the result of a voluntary agreement on the part of individuals to pursue their self-interests together.

Thirty years before Bellah, Eugene Nida wrote that "rather than selecting to emphasize social responsibility and community living, we have laid stress on 'rugged individualism' and a pattern of dog-eat-dog economic competition, which is no doubt efficient in bringing people more gadgets at less expense, but also brings incomparably more suffering at incalculably greater cost."[8] And five years after Bellah's book, Hauerwas and Willimon noted that "modern people usually seek individuality through the severance of restraints and commitments. I've got to be me. I must be true to myself. The more we can be free of parents, children, spouses, duties, the more free we will be to 'be ourselves,' to go with the flow, to lay hold of new and exciting possibilities. So goes the conventional argument."[9]

What does individualism look like in the light of God's Story? It appears inadequate as a basis for assuring the dignity and worth of individual persons. Coupled with other cultural values, individualism in North America tends to exalt the value and importance of only *some* persons. Those who are weak, disabled, or deformed do not rank with those who are strong, successful, and famous. Furthermore, in the light of God's Story, individualism is a lie. We are created, redeemed, and destined for life in community — a life sustained by God's commitment to us and our commitment to each other. Bellah and company have seen and shown the self-destructive power of individualism.

When we listen to sermons, we have the right to see where we live in our culture. As our culture is brought to the light of God's Story, we will see many times and places that call for the Yes, No, or Maybe of faith. Our culture idolizes success of almost any kind. But what about the radiant grace that makes life and all its riches gifts of God rather than our achievement? Our culture idolizes health; we are a therapy-preoccupied people. But how then can we find a meaningful

8. Nida, *Customs and Cultures,* p. 39.
9. Hauerwas and Willimon, *Resident Aliens,* pp. 64-65.

place for suffering — both the elementary suffering *from* disease and disaster and the higher kinds of sufferings *with* and *for* others? We are a consumer-dominated culture as television proclaims every day. But how long will it take us to see that stewardship of the planet and the sharing of resources is God's design for life? We are a racist society in which white skin provides a blank check for power and privilege. Racism comes in many shades. There is the old Southern kind that says "We don't care how close you get to us as long as you don't get too high." There is the old Northern kind that says "We don't care how high you get as long as you don't get too close to us." There is the recent kind that says "We don't care how high or close you get, as long as you become like us." But what becomes, then, of God's Story, which says that differences among people are not a curse that justifies the concentration of power and privilege among a select few, but are rather gifts meant to enrich and reconcile the family of God through service?

When we listen to sermons, we have the right to see our culture in the light of God's Story so that we may see how to live faithfully in it.

If we are to see our own culture (or subculture) in the light of God's Story, it is important that the church be engaged in cross-cultural experiences as a normal part of its shared life. Nothing helps us see our own culture better than seeing ourselves through the eyes of people from different cultures. As we bring our cultures to God's Story together, we will be enabled to see more clearly, enabled to avoid confusing our culture with God's Story. Lesslie Newbigin again helps us see that:

> All our reading of the Bible and all our Christian disciple-
> ship are necessarily shaped by the cultures which have

formed us. In Europe over the past four hundred years these cultures have been embodied in nations which have taken the place of God as the supreme reality, calling for absolute and total devotion. The fruit of that idolatry was reaped in two terrible wars. In that situation, the only way in which the gospel can challenge our culturally conditioned interpretations of it is through the witness of those who read the Bible with minds shaped by other cultures. We have to listen to others. This mutual correction is sometimes unwelcome, but it is necessary and it is fruitful.[10]

It will take careful and humble listening for it to happen. And no one can claim 20/20 vision when we read the Bible through the spectacles of cultures and then see our culture through the spectacles of God's Story. But it has happened, it happens now, and it can happen again — maybe next Sunday. For when we listen to sermons, *we have the right to see our culture in the light of God's Story.*

10. Newbigin, *The Gospel in a Pluralist Society,* pp. 196-97.

Don't Check the Yellow Pages

JIM AND SUE were traveling through the Midwest and decided to spend the weekend in an attractive, mid-size city. After visiting tourist attractions on Saturday, they decided they would attend worship at a church on Sunday morning. But where?

At their hotel they checked the Yellow Pages. They were astonished. There were about eleven pages of churches. Sue guessed that there were somewhere between eight and nine hundred churches listed. They were classified into such groups as Apostolic, Assemblies of God, Baptist (with several subheadings), Episcopal, Free Methodist, Holiness, Independent, Latter-Day Saints, Lutheran, Methodist, Pentecostal, Presbyterian (three kinds), Reformed, Roman Catholic, United Church of Christ, and more that they did not recognize.

But where would they worship?

They finally decided to choose a church by its location and time of worship. They wanted a church near the hotel that would begin worship at 11 A.M. That way they could sleep in, have breakfast, and still walk to church.

They did. The church happened to be a large assembly

that identified itself as "American Baptist." The sermon was the third in a series of sermons about the church. Midway through the sermon the preacher asked the people to read aloud the words of the ancient Nicene Creed which was printed in a way that made these words stand out in bold letters: **I believe one holy catholic and apostolic church.**

The words did not fit well with what they had seen in the Yellow Pages. There were many churches, some "holiness," some "catholic," and some "apostolic." But here in this Baptist church, they listened to the sermon and saw the church the way the old Creed said it: I believe one holy catholic and apostolic church.

If you want to see the church for what it is, don't check the Yellow Pages. Nor the church ads in the Saturday newspaper. If you want to see the church for what it is, you need to hear the testimony of the apostles that is echoed in the ancient creeds: the church is one, holy, catholic, and apostolic. When we listen to sermons, *we have the right to see the church in the light of God's Story.*

The secret of the church lies hidden beneath what shows in the Yellow Pages, the newspaper ads, and the pages of church history. We can see the church's secret only by faith, and faith comes from hearing.

Listen to James Daane:

> the church is a part of the message it proclaims. This is evident from the Apostles' Creed, in which the existence of the church is included *as a part of* the faith the church confesses and preaches. The church does not preach itself; the church preaches Christ. But there is no possible proclamation of Christ without proclaiming the existence of the church, for in preaching Christ the church cannot avoid

proclaiming that it is the Body of Christ. The church is so identified with Christ that a proclamation of Christ is unavoidably a proclamation of the existence of the church.[1]

If we do not hear the secret of the church, we will not be able to see it. We do not expect the state as an institution to recognize the secret of the church. Our governments in North America do the best we can expect governments to do in a pluralist society. They recognize churches as voluntary religious institutions that are aligned with charitable organizations in serving society. And the popular understanding of churches in our culture — and even among the churches themselves sometimes — is that they are marketplaces for buying, selling, or volunteering religious services. Only by hearing will we be able to see the truth about the church: it is one, holy, catholic, and apostolic. When we listen to sermons, we have the right to see the church for what it is in the light of God's Story in Jesus Christ.

Some Christian traditions distinguish between a visible church and an invisible church. The visible church is the one we see when we worship on Sunday, when we read the church bulletin about all the activities, when we read the newspaper ads or the Yellow Pages. The invisible church, they teach, is the church as it truly is in relation to Jesus Christ.

Such a distinction is helpful at first. It is an attempt to answer the question about why the church that we see in the teaching of the apostles is so different from the church we see on the corner. We may need to keep that

1. Daane, *Preaching with Confidence: A Theological Essay on the Power of the Pulpit* (Grand Rapids: William B. Eerdmans, 1980), pp. 6-7.

distinction around to help us answer that question — but only that question, and only for a little while.

The distinction between the visible and invisible church is finally misleading. It has been used to justify all sorts of sins and failures, and it ought not to be carried into our adult life. The truth is that we *can* see the church as one, holy, catholic, and apostolic if that is what we hear when we listen to sermons about the church. If believing comes from hearing, seeing comes from believing. And if we hear, believe, and see the church for what it is and are not content with the distinction between the visible and invisible church, it could change the agenda of nearly every church in North America.

To hear that there is one church is to hear the truth about Jesus. When we say, "I believe one church," we highlight a special aspect of our faith in Jesus the Christ. Because there is one Savior, there can be only one church. Peter said it: "there is salvation in no one else, for there is no other name under heaven given among men by which we must be saved" (Acts 4:12). Faith sees through the churches to the one church redeemed by the one Savior.

Faith in the one Savior's church functions in the Christian faith much in the way Israel's faith in one God functioned in the old covenant: "Hear, O Israel, the LORD our God is one LORD, and you shall love the LORD your God with all your heart, and with all your soul, and with all your might" (Deut. 6:4-5). What a scandalous confession in a world of many gods! It flies in the face of all the evidence. Israel's neighbors saw many gods behind the incredible variety of powers and events in nature and in history. Today our culture still shows a hunger to worship many gods — treasury bonds, muscle tone, soap stars, red

Ferraris, designer labels. But Israel hung on to what was made known: there is one God over nature, history, and all the nations. And the church stubbornly clings to its confession in spite of all evidence to the contrary: there is one church. Unless we hear, we cannot see.

To hear and believe and see that there is one church is to get a glimpse of the future. God's purpose in Christ is "to unite all things in him, things in heaven and things on earth" (Eph. 1:10). God's agenda is to restore unity to a creation fractured in the fall. To see the unity of the church is to get a glimpse of the future.

The church itself seems to have come apart especially since the Protestant Reformation. It has contributed more than its share to the disunity and chaos of God's broken family and world. But the future of the church in Christ is unity. The Spirit who brooded in the beginning to bring creation out of chaos has laid the foundations for reuniting all things in Christ. If Christ is the source of the one church, unity is its destiny.

When we listen to sermons, we have a right to see the vision of the one church in Christ and the meaning of belonging to it. Membership in the one church means that we can see unity as both a gift and a calling. The gift comes in Christ; the call is to show in the world what we are in him. When Paul wrote to the Corinthians that "you are the body of Christ, and individually members of it," he was describing the gift of unity and *prescribing* that they were called to be in Corinth what they were in Christ. For us as well as for the Corinthians, unity requires that we practice our gifts for the common good. For us more than for the Corinthians, it requires that we relativize our traditions lest they become barriers to unity rather than resources for serving. Sermons that show us the one church will call us to experience and express that unity as a sign of what God is doing in the world.

The church is also holy. "I believe one holy church." The creed sounds like a bad joke at this point. Where is the holiness of the church? The story of the church is replete with unholy beliefs and activity, from the disgrace of the crusades to the disgrace of the television evangelists. We lament the bad press the churches often receive from the news media, but it's my guess that if anything they tend to underreport the unholiness that is afoot.

Then where is the holy church?

It is right where the one church is: in Jesus Christ. To hear that the church is holy is to hear that Jesus is holy. Whatever holiness the church has, it has because of his holiness. Without seeing that he is holy, we cannot see the holiness of the church.

One of the elementary meanings of *holy* is "different." Jesus was different. The way he entered the world was different, the way he lived, died, and left this world were different. The secret of his life was his unbroken fellowship with his Father in heaven. His death was a freely offered sacrifice for the sins of the world. His resurrection was the evidence that his death had broken the power of death along with its cause (sin) and consequence (hell). Jesus was different.

But all of that differentness would remain out of our reach except for this one bit of news: he did it for us. In doing all that for us, he revealed the heart of God. Jesus, who belonged completely to God, gave himself completely for us. That made him different. That made him holy.

The church shares the holiness of Jesus in two ways. First, Jesus has sent out a call to the world to trust him and thereby receive the forgiveness of sins. That was the

Pentecost message of Peter to those who had crucified Jesus. To trust him is to turn away from religion. If religion is our own attempt to make it right with God, to save ourselves or justify ourselves, we are called to turn away from religion and trust him. Through trusting that he died and lives again *for us,* we receive the gift of holiness. We are, like Jesus, *different.*

Second, Jesus has sent us back into the world as his representatives *for others.* Trusting that he is for us, we are freed to live for others. Forgiven, we are free to forgive. Like the unity of the church, the holiness of the church is both a gift and a calling. We receive holiness from him, and we, by representing him in the world as witnesses, live and die for others.

When we listen to sermons, we have the right to hear and see the only holiness available to us in the world: the holiness of Christ. Hearing brings believing, and believing is seeing. Without that, the "one holy church" would forever remain a bad joke.

One holy *catholic* church. When we listen to sermons, we have the right to see that the church is *catholic.*

The church no more appears to be catholic than it appears to be one or holy. Is 11 A.M. to noon on Sunday still the most segregated hour in a typical North American week? Churches gather around their "own kind." In the flow of history, churches have institutionalized themselves around national origin, doctrinal traditions, social class, and common causes. A catholic church should be a gathering of people from many nations, including people whom the society calls rich, poor, strong, weak, educated, uneducated, able-bodied, handicapped, upper-class, middle-class, under-class. A catholic church might look like a mistake to some modern observers.

In an effort to make the language of the creed more intelligible and to avoid suggesting a possible connection with the *Roman* Catholics, some Protestant churches substitute the word *universal* for *catholic*. And yet the point and power of being called *catholic* is not merely that the church exists universally but that wherever it comes to life it has the gospel and grace to embrace all different kinds of people. It means that we are truly saved by God's *grace* and not by our race, place, or face. It means that we don't have to meet any racial, cultural, moral, educational, social, or religious conditions to qualify for receiving the grace of Christ by faith.

If we are to see that the church is catholic, we need to hear it. Faith comes from hearing, and believing is seeing.

To hear and see that the church is catholic is to hear something about Jesus Christ. The church is catholic because the church believes that salvation is by God's grace in Christ. Grace is a special kind of love. Grace is God's free decision to be God to us in spite of all that has happened. Grace is God's seeking and finding Adam and Eve in the garden when everything we had heard until then led us to expect that the story was over. Grace is God's call to idol-worshiping Abraham, promising to be God to him and his family for the sake of blessing all the families of the earth. Grace is God sending Jesus to be born in Bethlehem without the aid of human power or consent. Grace is Jesus praying for those who nailed him to the cross: "Father, forgive them, for they know not what they do." Grace is love that doesn't let go.

If we were saved by anything other than such astonishing grace, then the church could not be catholic; it could welcome and embrace only certain kinds of people who qualified. If we are saved only by the grace of God in Christ, then the church can only be catholic.

To hear that the church is one, holy, and catholic is not only to hear something about Christ; it is also to catch a glimpse of the future. The vision of St. John becomes our vision: "After this I looked, and behold, a great multitude which no man could number, from every nation, from all tribes and peoples and tongues, standing before the throne and before the Lamb, clothed in white robes, with palm branches in their hands, and crying out with a loud voice, 'Salvation belongs to our God who sits upon the throne, and to the Lamb!' " (Rev. 7:9-10). The church is destined to be catholic because its origins lie in God's grace in Christ.

Being catholic is both a gift and a calling. The gift is grace, and the calling is to live out and represent that grace in the world. When we move out beyond the expected relationships with "our own kind," we will experience our limitations. If we cannot speak Spanish or comprehend the African-American experience or identify with Asian-American values or understand the ways and hurts of Native Americans, we may find ourselves asking for mercy. The call for mercy is the way of faithfulness for the catholic church. When we know we are saved by grace, we are called to be catholic, and when we practice being catholic, we will know our need for grace.

In these days between the resurrection and the new creation, the church is called to raise visible signs of what it means to be catholic. Small as these signs may seem, they are tokens of who we are in Christ, and thus they are essential to the witness of the church.

When we listen to sermons, we have a right to see the church for what it is in Christ: one, holy, catholic, and apostolic.

But what can it mean today when we say that the church is *apostolic?* What do the apostles have to say about who we are or what we do? Churches are determined these days by their names and reputations as congregations and denominations. An elder in a Reformed church was heard to say that he would not object to a merger between his denomination and another "as long as we do not lose our name." Names and traditions shape who we are. Synods, conferences, and church headquarters determine the faith, life, and activity of the churches. The evangelical, ecumenical, and charismatic movements give us our identities. Most contemporary congregations seem more interested in survival or success than they are in what the apostles said and did. Are we apostolic? Do we even care to be?

The church is apostolic because its faith always depends on the testimony of the apostles. The church of all centuries has always been only one generation away from becoming pagan, and that one generation is the generation of the apostles. Their witness is the one indispensable link between the church today and our Lord Jesus Christ. There have been many links since the apostles, links that have formed the rich variety of Christian traditions. And each of us can point to many links in our own personal experience, forged by faithful evangelists, parents, pastors, teachers, and friends. All these secondary links could be mended if they were broken, but the church could not survive if the original link to Christ were broken. Because the faith and existence of the church depend on the unique witness of the apostles in this way, we say that the church is apostolic.

When the church is strong, favored, prosperous, and successful, it takes the witness of the apostles for granted and pays attention to more "urgent" agendas. There are more interesting and pressing pursuits than listening to the apostles. But in times when the church has been oppressed, persecuted, and distressed, it has turned again and again, huddling around candles in the dark, to hear the original witness of those who said, "we cannot but speak of what we have seen and heard" (Acts 4:20).

Being apostolic, like being one, holy, and catholic, is both a gift and a calling for the church. It is a gift because the faith and existence of the church is firmly rooted in what is given: the witness of the apostles. The church does not create its message; it receives it from Christ through the apostles. It is a liberating gift for the church to say with St. Paul that "what we preach is not ourselves, but Jesus Christ as Lord, with ourselves as your servants for Jesus' sake" (2 Cor. 4:5).

But being apostolic also entails a calling. We are called to go into the world with the message of the apostles for our time. The church listens to the apostles with one ear to be instructed, corrected, and guided. And the church listens in our world with an ear to hearing how, when, and where to speak the saving news we have heard through them. To be apostolic means to be sent as witnesses who have seen something and dare to tell the truth about it. Witnesses are people who "move from beholding to attesting, from seeing to saying, from listening to telling, from perceiving to testifying, from *being* a witness to *bearing* witness."[2] That is the calling of the apostolic church.

When we listen to sermons, we have the right to see what the church is in Christ so that we know what we are called to be in the world. Without hearing, we cannot see.

2. Thomas G. Long, *The Witness of Preaching* (Louisville: Westminster/John Knox, 1989), p. 79.

From the outside, churches may appear to be growing, successful, friendly, competitive, helpful, eccentric, and caring — but that is just what the Yellow Pages are telling us.

When we listen to sermons, *we have the right to see the one, holy, catholic, apostolic church in the light of God's Story.*

— PART IV —

. . . To Hear the Word of God

— 10 —

The Audacity of Listening

BRYAN AND MIKE had been rooming together at State since September. On a cold February Sunday morning Mike showered earlier than usual. Bryan sat up in bed staring.

"You sick?"

"No," Mike said. "I'm OK. I'm just going to church."

"Church?" Bryan said glancing out the window as though the word itself had disoriented him. "My God, is it Easter or something?"

"No. I just decided."

"What for?"

"I guess I want to hear the Word of God. That's what my dad always said he went for."

Bryan pulled the covers over his head as if he had heard enough for that time of day. Two hours later, Mike returned and found Bryan reading, which was about as unusual for him on a Sunday morning as it was for Mike to go to church.

"Well, did it happen?" Bryan asked.

"Did what happen?"

"Did you hear the Word of God like your dad said?"

"I don't know," said Mike, "but if what I heard is true, it would make a difference."

"What did you hear?"

"Later," said Mike. "I want to think about it for a while."

When Mike said the words, "I guess I want to hear the Word of God," he had spoken with a mix of cynicism and wonder. On the way to church, he was struck by the audacity of his dad's — and now his — words. To go to church to hear the Word of God seemed presumptuous and even audacious.

Thirty years ago Gene E. Bartlett wrote a book entitled *The Audacity of Preaching*. If claiming to speak the Word of God in human words is the audacity of preaching, then it is no more or less audacious to go to church in order to hear the Word of God.

If sermon listeners have rights that are rooted in pulpit responsibilities, then when we listen to sermons, *we have the right to hear the Word of God.*

If the whole idea of pew "rights" is a bit unsettling, then the assertion of this "right" seems as absurd as it is audacious. After all, the good news of God's Story is that God wants to "waste" his grace and gifts on prodigal sons and daughters who have used up all their rights and now live by his mercy. If we have no rights before God and, indeed, do not need them because he is so astonishingly gracious, how can we say that we have the right to hear the Word of God when we listen to sermons?

The claim here is not that we have rights before God but that we have rights before the pulpit. In his wasteful, prodigal goodness, God has entrusted his Story to the church and wants it told and heard. The church appoints some to be pioneer listeners to that Story, and they listen on behalf of the rest of the church and world so that all can hear. Responsibilities and rights are both gifts of God's grace. But if in grace God has assigned preachers the task of speaking his Word, then those who listen have a right to hear the Word of God.

The audacity of speaking and hearing the Word of God are evident when a church ordains people as "ministers of the Word." In the ordination liturgy with which I am the most familiar, the essence of which is common to many Protestant churches, the minister is handed the command of St. Paul to "preach the Word." The congregation is then asked, "Do you promise to receive the Word of God proclaimed by him?" And when the exhortations are given, the congregation is urged to "remember that through him God himself speaks to you." The audacity of it!

This audacity is not the exceptional claim of an eccentric cult. The claim to hear and speak the Word of God in human words goes back at least to God's meeting with Moses at the burning bush, where God said to him, "say this to the people of Israel . . ." (Exod. 3:14). God turned Isaiah the priest into Isaiah the prophet with these words: "go, and say to this people . . ." (Isa. 6:9). Jeremiah, the reluctant prophet, reports what happened to him: "Then the LORD put forth his hand and touched my mouth; and the LORD said to me, 'Behold, I have put my words in your mouth' " (Jer. 1:9).

The audacity of speaking and hearing God's Word in human words continued with Jesus. When he sent seventy disciples out on a mission, he said to them, "he who hears you hears me" (Luke 10:16). And St. Paul recalled the reception he received from some of the people in Thessalonica: "We also thank God constantly for this, that when you received the word of God which you heard from us, you accepted it not as the word of men but as what it really is, the word of God, which is at work in you believers" (1 Thess. 2:13).

The Protestant Reformers were as audacious as St. Paul in their claims about speaking and hearing the Word of God in human words. The Second Helvetic Confession is typical of what they believed: "Wherefore when this Word of God is now preached in the church by preachers lawfully called, we believe that the very Word of God is preached, and received of the faithful."[1]

The audacious claim continues today. It is heard in theologies today as richly diverse as those of James Daane, Elizabeth Achtemeier, David Buttrick, Sidney Greidanus, and Thomas G. Long. Buttrick warns that the claim can encourage an unwarranted arrogance, but he affirms it nonetheless:

> we are emphatically human, and we speak human words. Preaching must be described as a human activity that draws on human understanding and employs human homiletic skills that can be learned. Thus, though we preach knee-deep in grace, we can claim no status for our words. Gratitude, wonderment, a sense of inadequacy — all are preferable to status claims, particularly status claims for the words we speak.
>
> On the other hand, preachers should not lose track of mysteries in preaching, so that they regard sermons as human works of art or eloquence. Once more, we must modestly claim that preaching *is* "the Word of God." . . . So our ministerial vocation is peculiar. We are chronically

---

1. The Second Helvetic Confession, in vol. 3 of *The Creeds of Christendom*, 4th ed., ed. Philip Schaff (New York: Harper, 1919), p. 832.

bemused by our obvious inadequacy, our demonstrable humanity (we can live without the notion that we are professionals!), and, at the same time, staggered by being *chosen* to preach. Christ transfers preaching to us, and gives grace to our speaking, so that, odd as it may seem, our sermons are Word of God to human communities.[2]

Karl Barth once wondered, "Who dares, who can, preach, knowing what preaching is?" We can turn his wondering around: "Who dares, who can, *listen*, knowing what listening is?"

But we need to do more than merely say that when we listen to sermons we have the right to hear the Word of God. Do we have any clues to what makes this audacious claim possible?

One important clue is given to us in the words of the Apostles' Creed. The creed gives voice to our faith in "Jesus Christ, [the Father's] only Son, our Lord, who was conceived by the Holy Spirit and born of the virgin Mary." These words express our faith that Jesus the Christ is both God and human through the work of the Holy Spirit. That gives a clue to how it is possible for the sermon we hear to be both the Word of God and the words of a human preacher at the same time.

Jesus was fully human because he was born of the Virgin Mary. The virgin birth has long been used to argue that Jesus was divine. And yet it was not the virgin *birth* that was a sign of his divinity, but rather the virgin *conception*. In fact, the *birth* of Jesus from the womb of Mary is a sign of his full and complete *humanity*. Mary was fully human. Her humanness did not need to be revised or

2. Buttrick, *Homiletic: Moves and Structures* (Philadelphia: Fortress Press, 1987), pp. 456-57.

removed for her to be the mother of Jesus. Mary was who she was — a teenager from Nazareth, which is to say a nobody from nowhere that mattered. Her full humanness is a sign of the full humanness of Jesus.

However, according to the creed, the conception by the Holy Spirit is the sign that Jesus was the Son of God. Joseph was not present in the conception. Though it is not proclaimed in the creed, Joseph's absence from the conception is the sign that Jesus was the Son of God by the work of the Holy Spirit. Mary could do nothing to guarantee that the fruit of her womb would be the Son of God; only the Holy Spirit could do that.

That is our clue to seeing how it may be possible for the words of a sermon to be the Word of God. The preacher can do nothing that will *guarantee* that his or her words will be the Word of God. Only the Holy Spirit can do that. The stance of the preacher is that of Mary, who wonders how this can be. And when informed that this can be because of the Holy Spirit, the preacher says, "Behold, I am the handmaid of the Lord."

Another clue to seeing how the words of a sermon can be the Word of God is found in the connection between Christ and the Holy Scriptures. Jesus the Christ is the meaning and message of the Scriptures. He provoked the religious leaders with his words about the Old Testament: "you search the scriptures, because you think that in them you have eternal life; and it is they that bear witness to me; yet you refuse to come to me that you may have life" (John 5:39-40). And in the remarkable story of the risen Christ on the road to Emmaus, he spoke to his bewildered and despairing friends about himself from the scriptures: "beginning with Moses and all the prophets, he interpreted to them in all the scriptures the things concerning himself"

(Luke 24:27). So intimate is the connection between Christ and the scriptures that it is possible to say that if we know and confess Jesus Christ as Lord and Savior, we know the scriptures even if we cannot recite the books of the Bible — even if we cannot read.

And that connection between Christ and the scriptures, like the divine and human natures of Jesus, is provided by the Holy Spirit. St. Paul encouraged Timothy to continue in what he had learned and believed because the scriptures that instructed him in salvation through faith in Christ were inspired by the Holy Spirit (2 Tim. 3:14-16).

The Spirit who united the two natures of Jesus Christ and who unites Jesus Christ with the holy scriptures is the Spirit who makes possible this audacious claim: when we listen to sermons we have the right to hear the Word of God.

The claim is also humbling. Knowing that it is not we — preacher or listener — who can make the Word of God become a sermon any more than Mary could make the Word of God become flesh, we are put in our place. The place of trust is where we belong when we listen for the Word of God in the scriptures or in sermons. Such trust comes with believing that in Jesus the Christ the Word was made flesh for our salvation.

And the claim is encouraging. Just as we cannot guarantee that the Word of God will be heard in human words, we cannot prevent it either. In the fourth century the church debated whether the baptisms performed by priests who later defected under persecution were still valid. It eventually decided that they were in fact valid, because the validity of the sacraments does not rest in the person, the piety, or the virtue of the priest. The same is true of preaching and listening to sermons. The church and its preachers have had brilliant moments, but they have also had dismal streaks. Still, the Holy Spirit can bring the Word of God in human words even in the worst of times.

If the Word of God is heard in ordinary human words in a sermon, we should not be surprised to hear the Word of God in other ways and places. A song, a conversation with a friend, a letter, a classroom lesson — these may all be opportunities for the Spirit to use ordinary human words to enable us to hear the Word of God.

When we lived in Columbus, Ohio, there was a billboard near our house that featured a Volkswagen with a flat tire and the words "Nobody's Perfect." When our young daughter saw that sign as we were driving past, she laughed and said, "Guess that's like us, huh, dad?" She was hearing more than an ad for a car. The Spirit was making connections. She heard the grace that frees us to live with our imperfections. Did she hear the Word of God in those words?

The Spirit is free, but is there any order that can create the expectation that we will hear the Word of God when we listen to a sermon? It is one thing to say that we cannot *guarantee* that God's Word will be heard in the words of our sermon; it is another to say that we can do nothing to create the expectation that we will indeed hear the Word of God. Mary called herself God's "handmaiden." What can a preacher do as a handmaiden through whom the Word of God can be born in a sermon? Has the Spirit given us an order that can create the expectation?

The order the church has discerned in scripture and history is this: when an appointed person speaks from a Bible text to the world and life of the listeners, we can expect to hear the Word of God. I've worked to establish that point in the preceding chapter, but it deserves a summary look here to validate our audacious claim.

The person who speaks the sermon is appointed by the church to do so. Although orders by which churches authorize people to preach vary widely from, say, the independent "free" traditions to the Roman Catholic Church, every church has an order by which persons are appointed and authorized to speak in the name of the Lord. The differences among the orders need not concern us here. The point at issue is that the Spirit does in fact authorize people to preach through the order of the church. The authorization may be a lifelong commission or it may be for a limited time, place, or purpose. People do not become preachers without the recognition or consent of the church. And when they are appointed, the church has a claim on their gifts and can expect responsibility for carrying out the task of listening and speaking on their behalf.

Because the order and discipline of the church surround the preaching event, we can expect the Spirit to speak in a sermon in ways we do not expect otherwise, as Nicholas Wolterstorff has suggested:

> the church, in its official capacity, does what it can to insure that its preachers will indeed be speaking on God's behalf and not merely uttering personal fantasies. It requires that they attend an approved seminary, that they base their sermons on some passage in the Scriptures, that their preaching be within the church creeds and confessions, and that they willingly submit themselves to the discipline of the office-holders of the congregation. As the result of all this it seems to me that God characteristically speaks more emphatically, more incisively, more decisively, in the sermon than in casual sermon criticism. What I mean by that is that characteristically what God holds me concretely

responsible for on account of my having heard a sermon
is more expansive than what he holds me concretely responsible for on account of having heard some casual
sermon criticism. Because of that elaborate context of discipline surrounding the sermon, I am obliged by God to
take sermons more seriously than casual talk, as the bearers
of his very speech. *Characteristically.*[3]

The sermon is thus a kind of speech that creates the expectation that we will hear the Word of God.

The second element in the Spirit's order is that the
appointed person speaks from a Bible text. Paul did not
need Bible texts to preach in Lystra (Acts 14) or Athens
(Acts 17), but we are looking for patterns in the Spirit's
work that will create the expectation of hearing the Word
of God. A speech that depends on a Bible text for what it
says, means, and does is a speech in which we may expect
to hear the Word of God. Jesus, the Word become flesh,
has bound himself to the scriptures through his Spirit.
When a pioneer listener goes to the scriptures, listens with
the ears of the listeners for the Word of God, and then
speaks a message that was intended in that text, the Word
of God will be heard.

It is important that the sermon expresses the *intended*
message of the biblical text. Sermons may include many
Bible quotations, but if the message of the sermon was not
intended by any of the texts, then the sermon is not biblical,
and we cannot expect to hear the Word of God. The mere
reading of a Bible text does not make a sermon the Word
of God. The sermon must be authorized and shaped by the
message of the text.

3. Wolterstorff, "Are 'Bad Sermons' Possible? An Exchange on
Preaching," *Reformed Journal,* November 1977, p. 11.

The Spirit's order that creates the expectation that we will hear the Word of God is this: an appointed person speaks an intended message from a Bible text to the world and life of the listeners. That world, we have seen, is the world of our history, our culture, and our church. Those are the arenas in which we live, and those are the arenas in which we hear the Word of God.

Perhaps I can add a word here about what prepares us as listeners to hear the Word of God. We have already seen that the needs and experiences of life prepare us to listen and hear, but I would also stress that the witness and worship of the church itself prepare us. In Acts the apostles were living out their faith in the risen Christ, and when they spoke the mighty works of God on Pentecost, they evoked a question: "What does this mean?" (Acts 2:12). That question prepared the listeners to hear the Word of God. This pattern is evident throughout the book of Acts. The church lived and spoke its faith, there was a response in the form of a question or rejection, and then the Word of God was spoken and heard. The witness of the church continues to prepare us to hear the Word of God.

And the worship of the church prepares us to hear. Whether the worshipers are veteran believers or cautious newcomers, worship is a time and place in which we practice what we believe together. In the praise, prayers, readings, forgiveness, creed, and offering of gifts, being part of the community of faith that practices what it believes together can prepare us to hear the Word of God in the sermon.

We left Bryan and Mike in their dorm room after Mike returned from the church where he had gone to hear the Word of God. He had not yet told Bryan what he heard. He wanted time to think about it. But he did say that if what he heard was true, it would make a difference. To see and say that after hearing a sermon is to cross the threshold of faith.

Joseph Sittler has asserted that, "in a sense, that's what a sermon is for: to hang the holy possible in front of the mind of the listeners and lead them to that wonderful moment when they say, 'If it were true, it would do.' To pass from that to belief is the work of the Holy Spirit, not of the preacher or teacher."[4]

This is the audacity of faith: when we listen to sermons, *we have the right to hear the Word of God.*

4. Sittler, *Gravity and Grace* (Minneapolis: Augsburg Press, 1986), p. 63.

— 11 —

"Church Preaches to Church"

ON APRIL 8, 1945, Dietrich Bonhoeffer preached his last sermon in the schoolhouse that served as a temporary prison in Schonberg, Germany. He preached "without ornamentation, liturgy, or religious trappings for a few Protestants, Catholics, agnostics, and atheists."[1] After the closing prayer, he was summoned from the schoolroom with words that the prisoners knew led to the gallows: "Prisoner Bonhoeffer, get ready to come with us." Dietrich then spoke to his fellow prisoner Payne Best and said, "This is the end — for me the beginning of life." He was hanged the next day for resisting the Third Reich.[2]

How fitting that Bonhoeffer should have preached on that last day of his life. It is symbolic of a neglected side of his person and work — his love for preaching and listening to sermons. He is known for his endorsement of "religionless Christianity" and for rejecting "cheap grace," but these famous expressions tend to eclipse his love for the church and his devotion to the Word of God preached.

1. Clyde E. Fant, *Bonhoeffer: Worldly Preaching* (Nashville: Thomas Nelson, 1975), p. 4.
2. Fant, *Bonhoeffer,* p. 24.

Bonhoeffer also *taught* students to preach. In the seminary he helped found in Finkenwalde in 1935 to prepare preachers for the Confessing Church that opposed Hitler, Dietrich taught homiletics until the Gestapo closed the seminary in 1937. Even then, he continued to teach until he was silenced by government order in the summer of 1940. Some of his lectures are available to us and are filled with gems of wisdom and insight. In one of his lectures on preaching he said that

> everything hinges on the question of what the gospel is. Is it inspiration, education, conversion? Certainly it includes all of these things, but all under the one goal that the congregation of Christ might become the church. I preach, because the church is there — and I preach, that the church might be there. *Church preaches to church.* This means that I do not set a personal goal for myself to pursue, a goal of either inspiration or edification.[3]

What a strange statement! "I preach, because the church is there — and I preach, that the church might be there. Church preaches to church."

What do those words sound like in North America today? They sound self-serving at the very least. In our present situation, in which the church officially enjoys the favor of the state and has been granted tax-exempt status, "Church preaches to church" sounds like a call to mind our own business, to take care of ourselves and let the state run its own affairs in its own way.

But these words came from a teacher and preacher who was silenced by Himmler in 1940, forbidden to write or publish in 1941, sent to prison in 1943, and executed

3. Fant, *Bonhoeffer,* p. 138; italics mine.

in 1945. Is it possible that, rightly understood, these words of Bonhoeffer are subversive to the powers of evil? Can "church preaches to church" actually be revolutionary words that sound self-serving to us only because our favored status has put us out of touch with the reality of the evil that took Bonhoeffer's life?

If we were in trouble with the state, would we be able to understand Bonhoeffer's words? Perhaps Robert McAfee Brown is right: "the trouble with the church today is that the church is not in trouble."[4]

"I preach, because the church is there — and I preach, that the church might be there. Church preaches to church." There is nothing self-serving or world-fleeing in those words. Indeed, Bonhoeffer's passion was "to claim for Jesus Christ a world that has come of age." Translated into pew rights, Bonhoeffer's words mean that when we listen to sermons, *we have the right to hear the faith of the church proclaimed from the church, to the church, for the world.*

To see how the sermon is from the church, to the church, and for the world, recall how Jesus came from Israel, to Israel, and for the world, and how the scriptures came from the church, to the church, and for the world. The way the Word became flesh and the way the Word became scripture are clues to how the Word becomes a sermon in the church and for the world.

Jesus came from Israel. His life, preaching, and teaching took place in the first-century Jewish community in Palestine and were proclaimed as the fulfillment of the Old

---

4. Brown, quoted by James Daane in *Preaching with Confidence: A Theological Essay on the Power of the Pulpit* (Grand Rapids: William B. Eerdmans, 1980), p. 16.

Testament scriptures. When Jesus appeared as a stranger to two disciples on the road to Emmaus on the day of the resurrection, he began with Moses and the prophets and "interpreted to them in all the scriptures the things concerning himself" (Luke 24:27). And when the Ethiopian eunuch asked Philip a question about the meaning of words from Isaiah 53, "beginning with this scripture he told him the good news of Jesus" (Acts 8:35). Jesus came *from* Israel.

But Jesus also came *to* Israel. The Gospels disclose moments when Jesus was tempted to forsake his mission to Israel. In the wilderness temptations, Satan showed Jesus "all the kingdoms of the world in a moment of time" (Luke 4:5) and offered to give them to him. But Jesus became a different kind of king in and through his mission to Israel. When the Canaanite woman came begging Jesus to heal her daughter, Jesus spoke words that offend our modern sensitivities: "I was sent only to the lost sheep of the house of Israel" (Matt. 15:24). Her faith overcame Jesus' words, and he healed her daughter anyway, thereby giving a sign of the future when Christ's mission would be to *all* the nations. But the only way to that future was through his mission to Israel.

Jesus had opportunity to forsake Israel. Early in his ministry in the north country, in the city of Capernaum, Jesus became famous for his teaching and healing (Mark 1:28). His words and works made him popular enough for the people of Capernaum to extend a "call" to him to be their preacher. They wanted him to stay with them and care for their needs. Jesus had opportunity to settle down and become a successful religious leader, to start a new religious movement and live to a ripe old age surrounded by devoted followers.

But Jesus came from Israel *to* Israel. His response was faithful to his mission: "Let us go on to the next towns, that I may preach there also; for that is why I came out" (Mark 1:38). Capernaum called, but Jesus was on his way to Jerusalem and could not stay.

The Gospel according to John reports two encounters between Jesus and non-Israelites — both of which confirmed his mission to Israel. In chapter 4 we read that Jesus spoke to a Samaritan woman and disclosed to her that he was the Christ (4:26). Her witness brought Samaritans from the city to ask him to stay with them (4:40). Jesus could have become a successful religious teacher among the Samaritans who believed him to be the Savior of the world (4:42), but he moved on to Galilee and Jerusalem (5:1).

When Jesus entered Jerusalem for his final visit, there were Greeks present. They wanted to see him. They talked with Philip, who went to Andrew, and together they told Jesus. The news troubled Jesus. It meant that it was time for him to die. He could draw all people to himself only by being "lifted up" (12:32), and so he continued his course to the cross.

Jesus could have become a successful religious leader in Capernaum, or among the Samaritans, or with the Greeks, but he stayed his course toward Jerusalem because he had come for "the lost sheep of the house of Israel" (Matt. 15:24).

Jesus came from Israel to Israel for the world. The Gospels all announce his universal significance. By staying with his mission to Israel, Jesus became the Savior of the world. As the Lamb of God, he took away the sins of the world (John 1:29). By being lifted up on the cross, he drew all people to himself (John 3:14-15; 12:32). And the risen

Christ commissioned his disciples to go and make disciples of all the nations (Matt. 28:19).

Jesus stayed with his mission. He came from Israel, to Israel, for the world.

Similarly, the Scriptures came from the church to the church and for the world. The scriptures of both the Old and New Testaments came from the "church," the community of faith, and were meant to serve the community of faith. That community, in turn, was created to bring the blessing of Abraham to all the families of the earth.

Jesus came from Israel, to Israel, for the world. The Scriptures came from the community of faith to the community of faith for the world. Similarly, the sermon you heard last Sunday came from the church to the church and for the world.

Dietrich Bonhoeffer had it right: "I preach because the church is there — and I preach, that the church might be there. Church preaches to church."

The sermon comes from the church because Christ has entrusted the church with preaching the gospel. A sermon is spoken from the church's scriptures by the church's appointed pioneer listeners, nurtured and disciplined by the particular tradition out of which it arises, and it gives voice to the faith of the church. A sermon is not the possession or product of an elite few; it is the responsibility and privilege of the whole church.

Thomas G. Long has paid close attention to the way in which preachers enter the pulpit. He notes that in most churches, the preacher moves to the pulpit from somewhere *outside* of where the congregation waits. He understands that there are many good reasons for that practice, but wonders if it might obscure the important truth that preachers enter the pulpit from the pew:

What is at stake [here] is the more urgent matter of how worship leaders, including preachers, understand themselves and their leadership roles in relationship to the whole community of faith. . . . Preachers come to the pulpit from *somewhere,* and unless we can name that place, we risk misunderstanding who we are and what we are supposed to be doing in the pulpit. When we who preach open the sanctuary door on Sunday morning and find a congregation waiting there for us, it is easy to forget that we come *from* these people, not *to* them from the outside. We are not visitors from clergy-land, strangers from an unknown land, ambassadors from seminary-land, or even as much as we may cherish the thought, prophets from a wilderness land. We are members of the body of Christ, commissioned to preach by the very people to whom we are about to speak.[5]

When we listen to sermons, we have the right to hear the faith of the church because the sermon comes from the church. The gospel that gave birth to the church is the gospel that is echoed in the church's sermons. When we listen to such sermons, we will hear God's Story portrayed, our deepest needs addressed, the burdens imposed upon us by bad religion unloaded, and the testimony of the apostles resounded.

Some days the sermon may speak for us at a distance, depending partly on our life circumstances and partly on how closely we identify with the church and its faith at the time. At other times the sermon may speak for us with an immediacy that will fetch a silent "ah, yes" or a loud "amen!" from our souls. If the sermon comes from the church, we can expect sermons to speak the faith of the

5. Long, *The Witness of Preaching* (Louisville: Westminster/John Knox, 1989), p. 11.

church. If we are identified with the church, we can expect sermons to speak for us.

"Church preaches to church," Bonhoeffer said. Sermons are delivered *to* the church as well as *from* the church. The sermon has a message that stretches from the pew to the pew by way of the pulpit. To preach or listen to a sermon is to feel that tension as it speaks for us and to us.

Jesus lived and died in tension with the Israel from which and to which he came. The scriptures were almost invariably in tension with the communities from which and to which they were written. Sermons are heard in tension with the church from which and to which they are spoken.

Thomas Long sees the tension between the *from* and the *to:*

> the preacher rises from the pew and then stands in front of the people to preach. The preacher comes from God's people and thus is not outside the people or above them. But the preacher stands in front of the people because what the preacher is about to do is not of the people's own making or, despite all the work of sermon preparation, of the preacher's own making. As Moltmann puts it, "It comes from their God, in whose name they speak and act."[6]

Though the sermon comes from the church, the church is not the message of the sermon; the Word of God which created the church is the message. The church is identified with and by the message, but the church is never *identical to* the message. If the church is ever tempted to make itself the message out of a desire to succeed, compete, or even survive, we have the corrective word of St. Paul:

6. Long, *The Witness of Preaching,* p. 15.

"what we preach is not ourselves, but Jesus Christ as Lord, with ourselves as your servants for Jesus' sake" (2 Cor. 4:5).

The sermon speaks the faith of the church to the church because the church lives between what we were without Christ and what we shall yet become in Christ. Because of Christ the church has received a new identity, purpose, and hope, but it still suffers from amnesia, aimlessness, and despair. It needs to hear the news it has received and the faith it has confessed. The church needs what St. Paul reiterated for the church in Ephesus: "remember that you were at that time separated from Christ. . . . But now in Christ Jesus you who were once far off have been brought near. . . . So then you are no longer strangers" (Eph. 2:12-13, 19). When the church hears the words "remember — but God — so then," it is seized again and again by the new identity, purpose, and hope that come with living in God's Story.

Thomas Long, who knows that the sermon comes from the church, witnesses that it is also a word that comes to the church:

> so there we stand, we who somehow find ourselves in the pulpit with the commission to preach. We know, now, from where we have come, and it is from the congregation of Christ's people, both faithful and faithless, of which we are a part. They have taught us the "old, old gospel story" and have sent us now to this place to tell it anew to them; to recount its cherished word of hope; to remind them, because they have often forgotten, of its power; to call them, because they are prone to resist its claim, to take on once again its yoke which is easy and its burden which is light; to comfort them, because they are frightened and doubting, with its unfailing grace; and to reassure them that, no

matter how far they have strayed from home, it is still, and ever will be, the story of God with them and for them.[7]

The sermon is from the church, to the church, and *for the world*. Dietrich Bonhoeffer's life and death bear witness that when he said "church preaches to church," he was not calling the church to be introverted or self-serving. His driving concern was always "How can we claim for Christ a world which has come of age?"[8] He admitted no place to which the church might ever withdraw from the world. Rather, he insisted that the church exists *for* the world. Faithful preaching "places the church in the center of the village, and the cross in the center of the church; [preaching] sees the lordship of Christ . . . as the sustaining power of all reality."[9]

The church which preaches to church is in the world and for the world — as Bonhoeffer never wearied of saying. "The Church is nothing but a section of humanity in which Christ has taken form," he said.[10] One can hardly imagine a greater identification of the church with the world than that! And he taught that "the church . . . is to declare its liberating word to all of life; it exists for the sake of the world and stands at the point at which 'the whole world ought to be standing; to this extent it serves as deputy for the world and exists for the sake of the world.' "[11]

Church preaches to church *for the world*. For speaking and living that message, Bonhoeffer was executed.

7. Long, *The Witness of Preaching*, p. 15.
8. Fant, *Bonhoeffer*, p. 111.
9. Fant, *Bonhoeffer*, p. 111.
10. Fant, *Bonhoeffer*, p. 53.
11. Fant, *Bonhoeffer*, p. 90.

Preaching that is faithful to Christ for the sake of the world is *evangelical* preaching — that is to say, it announces the good news of what God has done for us in Jesus Christ. Bonhoeffer understood this to mean that the good news delivers us from "religion." If religion is a human attempt to bring God into the world and on our side to accomplish our purposes, religion is enslaving and futile. The gospel of Jesus frees us from religion for living Christ's life in the world. Bonhoeffer's opposition to "religion" is not as puzzling as it sounds at first. In the light of Jesus Christ, he saw religion — including Christianity when it is reduced to mere religion — as an impossible road from humanity to God. "Christ is not the bringer of a new religion, but the bringer of God. . . . So the gift of Christ is not the Christian religion, but the mercy and love of God which culminate in the cross."[12]

Preaching that is for the world is also *ecumenical* — not ecumenical in the limited sense of promoting church mergers but in the deeper sense of reconciling and reuniting God's broken family in one household. If in Christ God has broken down the barrier between Jew and Gentile, then surely all the other barriers that alienate people from one another cannot stand when that news is announced.

And preaching that is for the world is also *eschatological,* which is to say that it portrays the destiny of the world in Christ in ways that enable the church to practice the future *now.* Every sermon we hear should in some way be an echo of Jesus' introduction of his ministry: "the time is fulfilled, and the kingdom of God is at hand; repent, and believe in the gospel" (Mark 1:15). Living between the two comings of Christ, the church is propelled by the past and

12. Fant, *Bonhoeffer,* pp. 77-78.

pulled by the future to see and show signs of what his reign is like now. Sermons should help us sing doxologies that pull the future into the present. "For thine is the kingdom, and the power, and the glory forever."

"Church preaches to church," said the faithful witness Dietrich Bonhoeffer. And because the church is that part of the world in which Christ is formed, the church exists for the sake of the world. When we listen to sermons, *we have the right to hear the faith of the church proclaimed from the church, to the church, for the world.*

— 12 —

Come, Listen with Us

WHAT HAPPENS WHEN a church *calls* a preacher?

Martin E. Marty says that when a church calls a preacher or when people attend a preaching service, they are saying, "Preach to me." But just beneath the surface there is another plea:

> "Preach *with* me!" is the cry of the calling church. It has called preachers not to represent themselves. Instead they are to speak under the impulse of all the believers, for them all, to them all. And also to *each*. The called preacher has to represent me as someone who once had to come to faith from nonfaith. I am a participant in preaching whenever the words of someone authorized to use them helps others to grow, to come to new victories in a world of temptation. My growth in grace is a part of what the preacher displays through words from the Bible, which is now opened so that the ways of God can be disclosed in a new day. "Preach *with* me!"[1]

1. Marty, *The Word: People Participating in Preaching* (Philadelphia: Fortress Press, 1984), p. 15.

These words introduce a book written to help sermon
listeners participate in the act of preaching. Marty is right:
in the call of the church, preachers are asked not only to
preach *to,* but to preach *with* the listeners.

In a previous chapter I proposed another picture,
when I suggested that a church calls its preacher to be a
pioneer listener on its behalf. The church asks the preacher
to listen to the scriptures with its members' ears so that
they will be able to hear the saving Word of God. The
church says to the preacher, "Come, listen on our behalf."

But if Marty can hear the cry to "preach with us"
beneath the call to "preach to us," we can also hear the
cry to "listen with us" in calling a preacher to be a pioneer
listener. The church is straining to hear the Word of God
and summons the preacher to come and listen with them
so that together they can hear more clearly and faithfully.

But how does that happen? How does the preacher
"listen with" the church? Listening *with* involves listening
to the people so that when the preacher goes to the scripture texts, he or she can listen with their ears on their
behalf. Listening *to* them, the preacher can listen *with* them
when she or he listens to the text.

Listening with the people begins with listening to
them. People who listen to sermons *have the right to be
listened to before and after the sermons are spoken.*

If this right is respected, then people who listen to
sermons participate in their early formation. Supplying the
pioneer listener with needs, joys, fears, anxieties, hopes,
and life situations that call for a Word from the Lord, the
sermon listeners contribute to sermon preparation. If sermons are spoken from Bible texts to us, then sermons must
be found faithful at both ends: faithful to the Bible text
and faithful to those who listen. The sermon comes to life

when the preacher listens to the listeners and then listens to the text on their behalf. When sermon listeners are listened to, they contribute to the shaping of the sermons.

How can preachers listen to sermon listeners before and after delivering sermons so as to allow them to participate in the preparation of the sermons?

Such listening *to* is possible first because the preacher and congregation belong to the community of faith and have a variety of life situations in common. All experience the need for dignity, meaning, and hope (see Chap. 3), and they often share the circumstances that threaten dignity, meaning, and hope. The common life-shaping events of history bring them together to listen for each other's responses. Cultural, subcultural, and cross-cultural experiences can be shared in the community of faith that transcends them all. And their common membership in the church makes them brothers and sisters in a family that laughs, weeps, plays, prays, struggles, and rejoices together. Listening *to* is possible because of all that is common in the life situation that preacher and congregation share.

Listening *to* is aided by the pastor-congregation relationship of trust. Pastoral conversations, visits, counseling, and crisis intervention expose life situations that call for a word from the Lord. Pastoral privilege will of course preclude any violation of confidentiality in preaching, but this is not to say that pastoral experience cannot inform sermon preparation in powerful ways. Indeed, such experience can retune the preacher's hearing as he or she listens to the Bible text in order to prepare a faithful word for the people.

But the shared life situation and the pastoral relationship may not always be adequate for the kind of *listening to* that will bring sermon listeners into the early stages of sermon preparation. In our mobile, urban society, we tend

to associate with other people on the basis of common
interests, needs, and tasks — even in the church — and this
can render many of our relationships fragile and in-
complete. We are inclined to respect and prefer privacy in
all but the "safest" matters. When sermon listeners are
reluctant to share their experiences in this way, the preacher
will of course have a more difficult time participating in
it. In such a context, we may have to make special efforts
to ensure the kind of *listening to* that can begin to shape
sermons.

A number of people interested in the practice of preaching have stressed the importance of bringing preachers and
listeners into relationships in which the listeners can be
heard. John R. W. Stott recommends that the preacher meet
monthly with a group of approximately twelve persons from
various professions to discuss a book that they have all read
to gain some new insight into contemporary life. He has
derived much of value for preparing sermons by participating with such a group himself.

> The experience of the reading group — of the books we
> have read, the films and plays we have seen, and the
> discussion they have provoked — has not only increased
> our understanding of the modern world, but excited our
> compassion for human beings in their lostness and despair,
> confirmed our Christian faith, and rekindled our sense of
> Christian mission. I commend the value of such a group
> to all my fellow-clergy. There can hardly be a congregation
> in any culture, however small, which could not supply a
> few thoughtful people to meet with their pastor to discuss
> the engagement of the church with the world, the Christian
> mind with the secular mind, Jesus Christ with his rivals.
> The London group has given me the necessary stimulus to
> read at least some of the books I ought to be reading and

has provided me with some sharp-witted, warm-hearted young people as a congenial context in which to discuss the issues raised. They have helped to drag me into the modern world and have planted my feet on the soil of contemporary reality; I am very grateful to them.[2]

As a variation on that practice, Stott also gathered resource groups in preparation for a series of sermons entitled "Issues Facing Britain Today" in which he addressed such topics as unemployment, the arms race, and industrial relations. Before each quarterly sermon in the series, he met with a group of persons representing a wide variety of positions and interests to discuss the issue. They sought to relate biblical principles to contemporary life, and thereby participated in the early stages of sermon preparation. The practice illustrated and confirmed Stott's conviction: "at all events, I am convinced that there ought to be more co-operation between clergy and laity in the process of sermon-making, and that this is required by the New Testament picture of the Church as the multi-gifted Body of Christ."[3]

Merrill Abbey has written urgently and persuasively about the need for the preacher to bring the biblical text and present context together in dialogue. "Holding text and current experience together, he has the authentic insight of the one and the immediate urgency of the other. He is adrift neither from biblical authority nor from the recognizable life of the man in the pew."[4] Abbey describes

---

2. Stott, *Between Two Worlds: The Art of Preaching in the Twentieth Century* (Grand Rapids: William B. Eerdmans, 1982), pp. 196-97.

3. Stott, *Between Two Worlds*, p. 200.

4. Abbey, *The Word Interprets Us* (Nashville: Abingdon Press, 1967), p. 20.

a special series of sermons that Dow Kirkpatrick delivered on the subject of Christianity in daily work, in preparation for which he brought persons from similar occupations together for Bible study and discussion. "Before the sermon was preached, a spokesman for the vocational group made a five-minute statement about the problems as the group understood them. Out of this creative interchange came preaching both specific and Christian."[5]

These suggestions by Stott and Abbey point to the fact that the preacher and listeners share a responsibility for the sermon. This was also a matter of concern for Reuel Howe, whose study at the Institute for Advanced Pastoral Studies resulted in the publication of *Partners in Preaching* in 1967. His work with preachers and listeners showed that partnership can be practiced before, during, and after the hearing of the sermon. His plan for helping preachers listen to the listeners places emphasis on feedback groups that meet following the worship to answer prepared questions about the sermon.

Sidney Greidanus has also spoken of the importance of congregational involvement in listening to the sermon. The preacher can heighten such involvement, he says, "by aiming the sermon at specific needs in the congregation, by addressing the sermon, as the text before it, to specific questions. . . . But how can one meet the many, varied needs of a large group of people? Donald Miller compares preaching to shooting quail: 'If you aim for all the birds, you hit none, but if you aim for one, you are likely to get several.' "[6] But the aiming at specific needs does not begin

5. Abbey, *The Word Interprets Us,* p. 81.
6. Greidanus, *The Modern Preacher and the Ancient Text* (Grand Rapids: William B. Eerdmans, 1988), p. 184.

in the pulpit. It begins when preachers *listen to* the listeners who have called them to *listen with* them for the Word of God.

In churches where preacher and listeners already hear each other and thereby shape the sermons together, the old maxim applies: if it ain't broke, don't fix it. But if the space between the pulpit and pew has become soundproofed by distance or inattention, a plan for bringing the listeners into the early stages of sermon preparation can revive the experience of *listening with* each other.

Since the helpful works of Merrill Abbey and Reuel Howe were published in 1967, many plans and suggestions for how to involve the preacher and listeners in sermon preparation and response have been proposed. I developed my own plan in 1975, and it has proven helpful through limited use. I propose it here for whatever help it may give to others.

The heart of the plan is a daily diary prepared for use by a small number of sermon listeners each week. It divides the week between concerns specific to Sunday and concerns for the rest of the week. On each of the six weekdays, the sermon listener is asked to respond to two statements:

1. The following event, experience, thought, fear, question, doubt, or need was important in my life today.
2. The following words of faith or hope were important in my life today. (The words can be from the Bible, a hymn, a creed, a book, another person, or anywhere at all.)

On the page given over to Sunday, the listener is asked to complete four statements that relate to the sermon:

1. The sermon was about . . .
2. The sermon enabled me to believe that . . .
3. The sermon asked that I . . .
4. The sermon made me feel . . .

Though the diaries can be used in many ways to facilitate *listening to* the listeners, I would like to focus on two ways here. First, the pastor, an elder, or some other appointed person should be made responsible for enlisting volunteers who would be willing to keep the diary for one to four weeks. At any given time, no more than four persons should be keeping diaries, lest it become difficult to pay adequate attention to each of them. Each week the preacher should receive the completed diaries as a resource for reflection and for listening to the sermon text.

Volunteers should be informed of the purpose of the diaries and assured of the confidentiality of the content. One purpose is to help the pioneer-listening preacher to listen to the life experience of the listeners so that he or she can prepare faithful sermons in response. The diaries also help the preacher hear what the listeners *heard* in a previous sermon. Volunteers would also need to be assured that *one* entry per day is sufficient and that there are no right or wrong, good or bad entries. It would be quite acceptable to write that the most important event on a day was a flat tire that fouled up family plans or that a favorite basketball team pulled an upset. Indeed, such entries are much preferable to responses contrived to create a show of virtue, since the latter will not help the pastor's *listening to* or *listening with*.

The diaries should be received by the preacher at an arranged time. If they raise questions or concerns that need to be discussed, provision can be made for that along the way. At the end of the diary-keeping time — preferably a two- to four-week period — the preacher should meet with the volunteers to discuss the experience. As the effort proceeds, changes can be made to improve its usefulness.

The second way the diaries can be used is in a small group setting with the preacher presiding. Ideally, four persons would agree to meet with the preacher for one or two hours per week for four weeks, during which time they keep the diaries. During the meeting, the four participants would read their entries for the others following the sequence of the days. The group would take time to discuss the entries and whatever responses they evoke. The role of the preacher would be that of *listening to* so that he or she could be a *listener with*. At the close, the preacher would collect the diaries and distribute another set for use the next week.

The diary plan has many advantages. First, it can be adapted to many situations. The two ways I suggested can be revised to suit the life and composition of many different kinds of churches. The diaries are simple and easy to prepare. However the plan is used, the only wise rule is that no more than four persons should keep diaries at one time — whether they do so individually or as participants in a group.

Second, the plan offers a quiet, behind-the-scenes way to deepen the *listening to* in order to *listen with*. With regular use, the diaries and the pastoral interaction with the other participants promote healing powers gradually, more after the fashion of a prescribed medication than a major surgical procedure. The plan promises no quick-fix for major problems, but its benefits do accumulate over time.

Third, the plan effectively draws on the sermon listeners' area of expertise — namely, their experience of day-to-day life. It focuses attention on where people live and on what matters to them in that context. It taps into life stories and ignores neither the trivial nor the profound.

Fourth, the relationship of the preacher to the listeners is clarified as the plan is put into practice. As the sermon listeners see the preacher taking their eyes and ears to the sermon text, they get the sense that he or she is genuinely listening *with* them as well *to* them and *on their behalf*. No plan will sweep away all the ambiguities that surround the preacher-listener relationship, but this plan can help clarify the relationship. Wisely used, the diaries can improve both what is spoken and what is heard in the sermons.

Fifth, the diary keeping is educational. Individuals I have worked with in the plan have reported that after four weeks of making entries, they began to think about their life in terms of it. They found themselves asking — even when there was no diary to keep — what had happened that day that was really important and what words of faith or hope they had encountered. Some elaborate educational curricula would rejoice to accomplish that goal.

Finally, when the plan is practiced in the small group settings, relationships are deepened and caring takes place. Laughter, tears, wonder, appreciation, and understanding break open among the people. When men and women of various ages and races participate, barriers break down and new relationships are established. People are surprised by what they hear and see in the safe setting of the group. The caring that is generated carries over into other relationships in the church.

Churches call preachers to come and "preach with me," as Martin E. Marty has rightly noted. But churches also call preachers to come and "listen with us." People who listen to sermons have the right *to be listened to before and after sermons are spoken.* When that happens, preachers and listeners become listeners *with* one another.

Herbert F. Brokering's poem "Sermon" speaks a word for all seasons to people who speak and listen to sermons:

It was a sermon.
Not the best but the only one for this day.
I could have slept, with some of the others
But I did not.
I dared not.
I never do.
I had to stay ready, waiting and ready for his sentence.
Ready for the one sentence that was worth it all.
I always come to hear all of it for the sake of the one
    sentence.
All his preparing and all my listening is for the one
    sentence.
When he says it, I will hear it.
There are thought gaps.
Things he leaves out.
Space.
I fill in the gaps as he goes along.
What he does not say to us I say to myself.
He does not try to say it all.
He leaves blanks and spaces for me to fill in.
I do.
He does not know when he says his big sentence.
I know.
It's when all the words become one word.
When all the thoughts become one thought.
It's when the words become like flesh and blood to me.
My flesh and blood, Lord.

from *Uncovered Feelings* (Philadelphia: Fortress Press, 1969), pp. 24-25

Bibliography and Gift List

NOT ALL THE WORKS I have quoted or referred to are listed in this bibliography, nor are all those listed here used directly in the book. The standard of selection is that these books have been helpful enough to me in the preaching task during the past twenty years or so to merit a permanent place on my shelf.

All the listings relate directly to the task of preaching, with one exception. Lesslie Newbigin's *The Gospel in a Pluralist Society* is not about preaching, but it has profound implications for the message of the church in and beyond preaching.

The fact that I included Newbigin's book suggests that some of the most important books that nurture faithful preaching are not on the subject of preaching at all. But for the present purpose, I have limited the selections to that area with the one exception.

Since this book is for people who listen to sermons, this bibliography can serve as a gift list for people who preach sermons. To assist the reader who wants to shop, I have placed an asterisk by those titles that I would love to receive as a gift if I did not already own them.

160

Achtemeier, Elizabeth. *Creative Preaching.* Nashville: Abingdon Press, 1980.

Best, Ernest. *From Text to Sermon.* Atlanta: John Knox Press, 1978.

*Brueggemann, Walter. *Finally Comes the Poet.* Minneapolis: Fortress Press, 1989.

Buechner, Frederick. *Telling the Truth: The Gospel as Tragedy, Comedy, and Fairy Tale.* New York: Harper & Row, 1977.

*Buttrick, David. *Homiletic: Moves and Structures.* Philadelphia: Fortress Press, 1987.

Cox, James W. *A Guide to Biblical Preaching.* Nashville: Abingdon Press, 1976.

*Craddock, Fred B. *Preaching.* Nashville: Abingdon Press, 1985.

———. *Overhearing the Gospel.* Nashville: Abingdon Press, 1978.

Daane, James. *Preaching with Confidence: A Theological Essay on the Power of the Pulpit.* Grand Rapids: William B. Eerdmans, 1980.

Fant, Clyde E. *Bonhoeffer: Worldly Preaching.* Nashville: Thomas Nelson, 1975.

———. *Preaching for Today.* New York: Harper & Row, 1975.

*Greidanus, Sidney. *The Modern Preacher and the Ancient Text.* Grand Rapids: William B. Eerdmans, 1988.

Jensen, Richard A. *Telling the Story.* Minneapolis: Augsburg, 1980.

Keck, Leander E. *The Bible in the Pulpit.* Nashville: Abingdon Press, 1978.

Killinger, John. *Fundamentals of Preaching.* Philadelphia: Fortress Press, 1985.

Lewis, Ralph L., and Gregg Lewis. *Inductive Preaching.* Westchester, Ill.: Crossway Books, 1983.

*Long, Thomas G. *Preaching and the Literary Forms of the Bible.* Philadelphia: Fortress Press, 1989.

*———. *The Witness of Preaching.* Louisville: Westminster/John Knox, 1989.

*Lowry, Eugene. *The Homiletical Plot.* Atlanta: John Knox, 1980.

Lueking, F. Dean. *Preaching: The Art of Connecting God and People.* Waco, Tex.: Word Books, 1985.

Markquart, Edward F. *Quest for Better Preaching.* Minneapolis: Augsburg, 1985.

*Miller, Donald G. *The Way to Biblical Preaching.* Nashville: Abingdon Press, 1957.

*Newbigin, Lesslie. *The Gospel in a Pluralist Society.* Grand Rapids: William B. Eerdmans, 1989.

Nichols, J. Randall. *Building the Word: The Dynamics of Communication and Preaching.* San Francisco: Harper & Row, 1980.

Sanders, James A. *God Has a Story Too.* Philadelphia: Fortress Press, 1979.

*Stott, John R. W. *Between Two Worlds.* Grand Rapids: William B. Eerdmans, 1982.

Thielicke, Helmut. *The Trouble with the Church.* New York: Harper & Row, 1965.

Troeger, Thomas H. *Creating Fresh Images for Preaching.* Valley Forge, Pa.: Judson Press, 1982.

Thompson, William D. *Preaching Biblically.* Nashville: Abingdon Press, 1981.

Wilson, Paul Scott. *Imagination of the Heart.* Nashville: Abingdon Press, 1988.